XNA® 3.1 GAME DEVELOPMENT FOR TEENS: GAME DEVELOPMENT ON THE PC, XBOX 360®, AND ZUNE® PLAYER

JERRY LEE FORD, JR.

Course Technology PTR
A part of Cengage Learning

COURSE TECHNOLOGY
CENGAGE Learning™

Australia • Brazil • Japan • Korea • Mexico • Singapore • Spain • United Kingdom • United States

COURSE TECHNOLOGY
CENGAGE Learning™

XNA® 3.1 Game Development for Teens: Game Development on the PC, Xbox 360®, and Zune® Player
Jerry Lee Ford, Jr.

Publisher and General Manager, Course Technology PTR: Stacy L. Hiquet

Associate Director of Marketing: Sarah Panella

Manager of Editorial Services: Heather Talbot

Marketing Manager: Jordan Castellani

Senior Acquisitions Editor: Emi Smith

Project Editor: Jenny Davidson

Technical Reviewer: Keith Davenport

Teen Reviewer: JT Hiquet

Interior Layout Tech: MPS Limited, A Macmillan Company

Cover Designer: Mike Tanamachi

Indexer: Sharon Shock

Proofreader: Sara Gullion

XNA, Xbox 360, and Zune Player are all registered trademarks of Microsoft Corporation.
All other trademarks are the property of their respective owners.
All images © Cengage Learning unless otherwise noted.

Library of Congress Control Number: 2009933299

ISBN-13: 978-1-4354-5438-5

ISBN-10: 1-4354-5438-3

Course Technology, a part of Cengage Learning
20 Channel Center Street
Boston, MA 02210
USA

Cengage Learning is a leading provider of customized learning solutions with office locations around the globe, including Singapore, the United Kingdom, Australia, Mexico, Brazil, and Japan. Locate your local office at: **international.cengage.com/region**

Cengage Learning products are represented in Canada by Nelson Education, Ltd.

For your lifelong learning solutions, visit **courseptr.com**

Visit our corporate website at **cengage.com**

Printed by RR Donnelley Owensville, Missouri 1st Ptg. 01/2010

Printed in the United States of America
1 2 3 4 5 6 7 12 11 10

To my mother and father for always being there, and to my wonderful children, Alexander, William, and Molly, and my beautiful wife, Mary.

ACKNOWLEDGMENTS

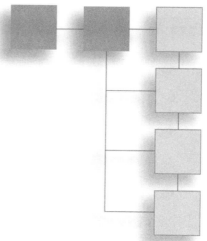

This book represents the hard work of a great many individuals to whom I owe many thanks. Special thanks go to Emi Smith. As acquisitions editor, Emi helped make this book a reality and ensured that things went smoothly. I also need to thank Jenny Davidson, who served as this book's project editor. Jenny's guidance and editorial skills were essential to the success of this book. Thanks also need to go out to the book's technical editor, Keith Davenport, who provided many invaluable insights and a great deal of technical advice. Last but not least, I would like to thank everyone else at Course Technology PTR for all their contributions and hard work.

ABOUT THE AUTHOR

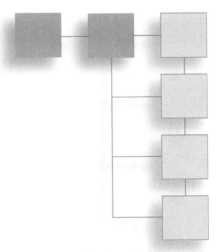

Jerry Lee Ford, Jr. is an author, educator, and an IT professional with over 20 years of experience in information technology, including roles as an automation analyst, technical manager, technical support analyst, automation engineer, and security analyst. He is the author of 33 books and co-author of two additional books. His published works include *Getting Started with Game Maker, DarkBASIC Programming for the Absolute Beginner, Scratch Programming for Teens, Microsoft Visual Basic 2008 Express Programming for the Absolute Beginner*, and *Phrogram Programming for the Absolute Beginner*. Jerry has a master's degree in business administration from Virginia Commonwealth University in Richmond, Virginia, and he has over five years of experience as an adjunct instructor teaching networking courses in information technology.

Contents

INTRODUCTION

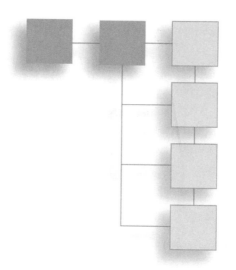

Welcome to *XNA 3.1 Game Development for Teens*! XNA Game Studio 3.1 is an integrated development environment (IDE) extension to Microsoft Visual Studio. Microsoft created XNA Game Studio 3.1 with one purpose in mind, to facilitate the development of computer games. Using Microsoft XNA Game Studio 3.1 you can create your own computer games and run them on your computer. If you have a Zune portable media player or an Xbox 360, you can run your games there as well. If you want, you can even sell your computer games on Xbox Live!

XNA Game Studio 3.1 relies on the XNA Framework. This framework provides a basic template for all new games, which includes access to resources needed to facilitate game execution. XNA Game Studio 3.1 provides you with everything needed to create professional quality computer games of all types and even supports the development of network games. Best of all, XNA Game Studio 3.1 does not require you to have an advanced degree in computer science to use it.

This book will provide everything you need to know to get up and running with XNA Game Studio 3.1 and Microsoft Visual C# 2008 Express, the programming language you will learn how to use when developing computer games. Using step-by-step, hands-on instruction, you will learn how to create all sorts of games and small programs, complete with graphics and sound effects. You will find that XNA Game Studio 3.1 provides everything you need to create professional-quality computer games. Once created, you can even market your games on Xbox Live.

XNA Game Studio 3.1 supports both 2D and 3D game development. This book will focus on 2D development, since it is easier to get started. You'll be given the skills and knowledge that you need should you later decide to jump into the world of 3D game development. Whether you are just getting started or are interested in finding out how to create and market the world's next game, XNA Game Studio 3.1 and this book will suit your needs well.

Why XNA 3.1?

Together XNA Game Studio 3.1 and Microsoft Visual C# 2008 Express provide an intuitive development environment that supports the creation of computer games. They provide everything needed to create, test, run, and debug computer games on a Windows computer. XNA Game Studio 3.1 supplies access to an enormous collection of pre-written program code, which you can call upon to simplify game development. This allows you to create professional-quality computer games, which you can then distribute and even sell royalty-free to other Windows and Zune users. In addition, if you elect to sign up with Xbox Live, you can sell Xbox 360 versions of your games.

Examples of the games that you can create include:

- Classic arcade games like *Space Invaders*, *Asteroids*, and *Missile Command*

- First-person shooter games like *Doom* and *Call of Duty*, and third-person shooters like Atari's original *Tank* game

- Maze games like *Pac-man* and *Ms. Pac-man*

- Multiple-player games like *Monopoly* or *Warcraft*

- Strategy games like the *Command and Conquer* series

- Network games that can be played on a home network or over the Internet like *Star Wars Galaxies*

- Sports games like classic Atari *Pole Position* racing game or *NBA Live 2009*

Of course, XNA Game Studio 3.1 doesn't limit you to the types of games listed above. You can use it to create pretty much any type of game you can imagine.

Who Should Read This Book?

XNA 3.1 Game Development for Teens has been designed to meet the needs of those gamers who love playing games and who want to make the leap from player to game developer. As this book will show you, playing games is fun, but creating your own games is where the real action and fun is. This book will not only teach you how to use XNA Game Studio 3.1 and Microsoft Visual C# 2008 Express to create all sorts of different games, but it will also teach you good programming about good game development principles.

XNA Game Studio 3.1 is easy enough for beginners to use to get started while at the same time is powerful to meet the need of advanced game developers. In fact, it provides everything you need to make the most advanced professional-looking games, everything that is except for the graphic and audio files that you will also need to give your applications the right look and feel. Fortunately, even if you are not a graphic artist or an audio engineer or musician, you will find there is no shortage of multimedia content available on the Internet.

As this book will show you, thanks to XNA Game Studio 3.1, game development is no longer the exclusive domain of veteran programmers with computer science degrees and decades of experience. While previous programming experience is certainly helpful, first-time game developers only require a good understanding of Microsoft Windows to get started. If you know how to operate a computer and are comfortable working with applications like Microsoft Office, you'll be surprised how quickly you will pick things up.

Advanced game developers, on the other hand, will be pleased to know that XNA Game Studio 3.1's game framework provides all of the programming power required to develop even the most complex games. It can be used to create stand-alone and network games. Whether you are just interested in having a little fun or you want to create and sell the next great Xbox 360 game, XNA Game Studio 3.1 will fit your needs quite nicely. With this book and a little time and effort you'll be creating all kinds of games and perhaps even taking your first steps in a new career in no time at all.

What You Need to Begin

XNA Game Studio 3.1 is free and so is Microsoft Visual C#, the programming languages that you will use when developing XNA games and applications. These are the only resources that you will need to begin developing games for execution on Windows and the Zune portable media player. XNA games are supported on any type of Zune player. However, if you want to make your games available for execution on the Xbox 360, your Xbox 360 will have to be connected to Xbox Live and you will have to sign up for an XNA Creators Club membership. Also, your Xbox 360 must also be equipped with a hard drive to store your games.

Since almost all of the program code that you will develop is portable to both the Xbox 360 and Zune execution platforms, this book will demonstrate XNA game development on Microsoft Windows. XNA Game Studio 3.1 works with any of the following versions of Microsoft Windows.

- **Windows XP with Service Pack 2** (Home Edition, Professional Media Center Edition, Tablet PC Edition)

- **Windows Vista** (Home Basic, Home Premium, Business, Enterprise, Ultimate)

All of the figures and examples presented in this book are shown using XNA Game Studio 3.1, running on Microsoft Windows Vista. Later in the book, you will learn how to port your games over to the Xbox and Zune player and to make any required adjustments to your program code. If your computer has a different version of Windows installed, you may notice small differences in how things look. However, all basic features and functionality work exactly the same.

Hint

Full support for XNA Game Studio 3.1 on Windows 7 is expected. XNA Game Studio 3.1 will install on Windows Server 2003 and 2008. However, it is not officially supported on either of these operating systems and may not operate as expected.

In order install and operate XNA Game Studio 3.1, your computer must meet the minimum hardware requirements listed in Table I.1. However, for good performance, you will want to make sure that your computer meets the recommended requirements.

In addition to the hardware requirements listed in Table I.1, your computer will require a graphics card that supports Shader Model 1.1 or higher and DirectX 9.0c. *DirectX* is a Microsoft technology that facilitates the development and execution of high-performance graphics and audio applications. Unless your computer is more than several years old, it should meet these requirements. If this is not the case, you can download and install it by visiting http://www. microsoft.com/windows/directx.

Table I.1   Minimum Requirements for XNA 3.1

Requirement	Minimum	Recommended
Processor	1.6 GHz	2.2 GHz
Memory	192 MB	384 MB
Hard Disk	5400 RPM hard disk	7200 RPM hard disk
Disk Space	1.3 GB free space	1.3 GB free space

Note: On Windows Vista you'll need a 2.4 GHz processor and 768 MB of memory.

As previously stated, game development using Microsoft XNA Game Studio 3.1 requires that you install Microsoft Visual C# 2008 Express Edition or Visual Studio 2008 Professional Edition. Microsoft Visual C# 2008 Express Edition is free and is the version that will be used throughout this book. You can download Microsoft Visual C# 2008 Express Edition at http://www.microsoft.com/express/vcsharp/.

Trap

Microsoft XNA Game Studio 3.1 is not compatible with versions of Visual Studio prior to 2008. If you are using an older version, you'll need to upgrade it to 2008 before installing Microsoft XNA Game Studio 3.1.

Assuming your computer meets the hardware and software requirements previously outlined, all you need to get started developing your own games is this book. Of course, if you want to develop games for the Xbox 360 or the Zune, you will need access to these devices.

Conventions Used in This Book

This book uses a number of conventions in order to make it easier for you to read and work with the information that is provided. These conventions are as follows.

Hint

Tips for doing things differently and things that you can do to become a more proficient XNA programmer.

Trap

Areas where problems are likely to occur and advice on how to stay away from or deal with those problems, hopefully saving you the pain of learning about them the hard way.

Trick

Programming shortcuts designed to help make you a better and more efficient programmer.

Companion Website Downloads

You may download the companion website files from www.courseptr.com/downloads.

Part I

XNA Development Basics

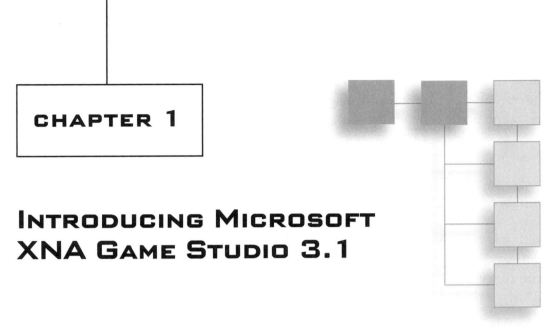

CHAPTER 1

Introducing Microsoft XNA Game Studio 3.1

Today computer video games are played on personal computers, portable devices, and game consoles. Computer games can be played solo or multiplayer and they can be played over networks like the Internet. Computer games pit players against each other or the computer in a make-believe world. Playing computer games can be a lot of fun. However, as this book will show you, making computer games is even more fun and challenging. Microsoft XNA Game Studio 3.1 provides a free game development framework that greatly simplifies the game development process. This chapter will provide an introduction to XNA game development and will give you a basic overview of how it is used to create new computer games.

The major topics covered in this chapter include:

- An overview of the key components and supporting technologies that make XNA work

- Learning how to set up your game development environment

- Learning how to create and execute your first XNA application

The Computer Gaming Industry

From its beginnings back in the early 1970s with relatively simple games like *Pong* and then later games like *Space Invaders*, *Asteroids*, and *Missile Command*, to the

3

newest generation of video games played on game consoles, computer gaming has become big business. Today's games like *Call of Duty* and *Guitar Hero* are reaching out to new generations of gamers. Game play has evolved from the early days of single-player computer games to games that can now be played over the Internet involving hundreds or thousands of players from around the world.

This new generation of computer games is played on powerful personal computers or on highly advanced game consoles, most notably the Xbox 360. Video games are often played on portable devices like Microsoft's Zune media player. Microsoft XNA Game Studio 3.1 is a new game development environment designed to help game developers create new generations of computer games that run on personal computers running Microsoft Windows, the Xbox 360, and the Zune media player.

Learning how to create video games using Microsoft XNA Game Studio 3.1 is a great way to get started as a game developer. Today, the video game industry generates more than $10 billion in revenues every year. There is a great need for talented game developers. In an effort to satisfy some of this demand, colleges and universities like ITT Technical Institute and DeVry and many others have created new degree programs in video game development and design.

If video game development sounds interesting to you, whether as a hobby or as a possible career, then learning how to create computer games with XNA Game Studio 3.1 is a perfect place to start, and there is no better way to get started than by reading this book and following along with and re-creating the sometimes silly and wacky programming examples and computer games that are presented.

Hint

To help you set your expectations as you read this book, it is important that you understand that today most of the computer games being sold are developed by large teams of professional programmers, graphic artists, audio technicians, and project managers who may work together for months or years with multi-million dollar budgets. There are, however, opportunities for individual game developers and small teams of developers with modest budgets. Game portals like Big Fish Games (www.BigFishGames) and Xbox Live Marketplace are opening new avenues of opportunity for game developers at all levels.

The purpose of this book is to teach you how to create computer games using Microsoft XNA Game Studio 3.1. You will also learn how to program using C#. This book does not, however, attempt to teach you about graphic design or sound and music development. These disciplines can take years to master. As you will find out, you can create some really good games using relatively simple graphics. In addition, you will find no shortage of free or low-cost graphics and audio files available on the Internet, which you can use to develop some pretty impressive looking games all by yourself.

Getting to Know Microsoft XNA Game Studio 3.1

To the average person, computer programming and game development is a mysterious and complex process that can only be performed by highly experienced programmers with years of education and training. While that was once the case, it is not that way any more. A new generation of development tools have appeared that are designed to simplify the development of computer games. One of these new tools is Microsoft XNA Game Studio 3.1.

Hint

Going forward, this book will use the term XNA when referring to Microsoft XNA Game Studio 3.1.

Microsoft created XNA for one reason, to simplify the creation of new computer games that can be run on a personal computer, the Xbox 360, and the Zune media player. XNA supports both 2D and 3D game development. While it does provide limited support for 3D game development, it is in the area of 2D development that it really shines. XNA greatly simplifies the development of games like *Space Invaders*, *Asteroids*, *Breakout*, and a host of related arcade-style games.

While 3D games represent the current state of the art in video games, new 2D games are still very popular and are being released all the time. Examples of popular 2D games include titles like *Odin's Sphere*, *Super Street Fighter Turbo*, and the *Command and Conquer* series. 2D games are easier to develop, especially for first-time game developers. As such, this book's focus will be on the development of 2D applications.

XNA 3.1 Uncovered

XNA provides a sophisticated framework that is specifically designed to support the development of computer games. This framework is made up of a number of different components, including:

- The Visual Studio or Visual Studio Express IDE

- The XNA framework

- DirectX

- C#

- The .NET Framework

The Visual Studio Express IDE

The programming language that is used in this book to develop XNA games is Microsoft C# 2008 Express. C# programs are created using the Visual Studio or Visual Studio Express *integrated development environment* or *IDE*. An IDE is an application that supplies all of the software tools needed to develop an application's program code. An IDE also provides the ability to execute programs and to debug them when errors occur.

Figure 1.1 shows an example of how the Visual Studio Express IDE looks when using C# to develop a new XNA game. As you can see, the IDE looks like a typical window application in a number of ways. For example, at the top of the IDE you will find a menu and toolbars. Beneath them is a code editor window and a

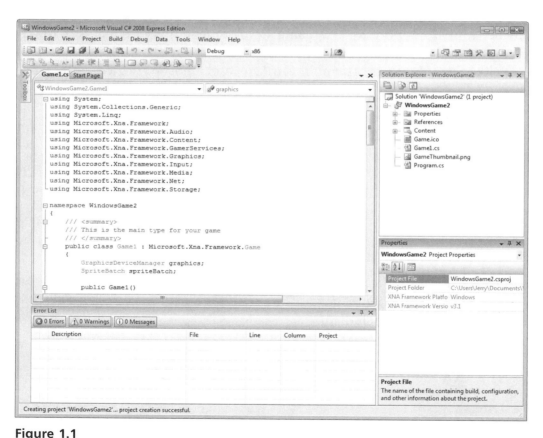

Figure 1.1
The Visual Studio 2008 Express IDE provides the working environment within which you will create and execute your XNA games using C#.

number of other windows that report error information and provide access to various project components.

As you will learn in Chapter 2, "Getting Started," the Visual Studio Express IDE is made up of a number of windows and a code editor that provides everything needed to create program code and to manage the graphics and sound files that make up your XNA games.

XNA Framework

XNA provides a framework designed specifically to support the execution of computer games. The framework provides the core functionality required to render graphics and manage game execution. It automatically handles tasks like:

- The execution of sound effects and the playback of background music

- Managing graphic animation

- The execution of special effects

- Determining when objects collide

- The provision and execution of core game code available through the framework's class library

Though different in many ways, all computer games share a common set of functionality. They collect player input, draw graphics on the display, execute graphic animation and sound effects, etc. The XNA framework simplifies game development by managing common components of all games. This allows game developers to focus on the development and design of features unique to their games. By working with the XNA framework, game developers save themselves the time and effort that would otherwise be required to create games from scratch. This significantly increases the amount of time and effort required to develop new games and results in games that are more reliable and easier to maintain.

XNA provides a large collection of pre-written programs (in the form of methods) that you can call upon in your computer games. These methods are designed to perform specific tasks. As you will learn, these methods provide your games with everything needed to display graphics, manage audio playback for sound effects and background music, and to detect and manage game interaction. To accomplish all this, XNA relies on another Microsoft technology called DirectX, discussed in the next section.

DirectX

DirectX enables the execution of commands that manage graphics and audio. It alleviates the requirement of having to work directly with hardware devices. DirectX handles all interaction with computer hardware like the gamepad, mouse, and keyboard as well as sound and video graphic cards. As you might imagine, learning how to work with DirectX is not easy. However, thanks to XNA, you do not have to deal directly with DirectX. The XNA framework handles all interactions with DirectX for you.

XNA leverages the capabilities of DirectX to simplify game development. As depicted in Figure 1.2, XNA simplifies game development by providing a wrapper around DirectX.

Hint

DirectX has been around since 1995. Since then, Microsoft has released a number of different versions of DirectX. As of the writing of this book, DirectX 10 was the most current version. However, XNA utilizes DirectX 9. DirectX 10 comes supplied with Microsoft Vista. Fortunately, DirectX 9 can happily coexist with other DirectX versions.

C#

The XNA framework provides an *object-oriented* programming environment in which games are created by defining objects that represent different characters.

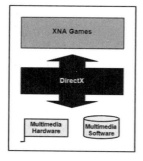

Figure 1.2
XNA 3.1 utilizes DirectX 9 and will automatically install it if it is not present or if a previous version is installed on your computer.

To interact with and control this environment, you need to learn how to program using C#. Microsoft Visual C# (pronounced C Sharp) is the Microsoft implementation of the C# programming language. C# is regarded as a general-purpose programming language based largely on C++ syntax. Microsoft created it as part of its .NET initiative. It is one of several languages supported by Visual Studio. Visual C# is also the primary program language used in the development of XNA games.

Using C#, you can bring life to your games, control how the game characters interact with one another, and respond to the different events that occur during game play. C# is syntactically similar to the C++ programming languages. C# is a compiled programming language. C# program code is compiled into an executable format at development time. This allows C# programs to start and begin executing the moment they are started.

Hint

Going forward, this book will use the term C# when referring to Microsoft Visual C# 2008 Express.

C# supports the same set of programming features found in most modern programming languages. This includes things like variables, arrays, conditional logic, and loops. Once you have learned C#, it will be easier for you to learn other programming languages like C++ and Java, which are used by professional game developers to create many of today's most popular games. C# is covered in depth in Chapters 3–5.

The .NET Framework

The .NET Framework is a key component in most Microsoft applications. It supports the creation and execution of desktop, network, and Internet-based applications. A special version of .NET, known as .NET CF, also supports the development of applications for portable devices like the Zune player. XNA uses .NET Framework. A good understanding of .NET 2.0's major components and services is essential.

All of Microsoft's Visual Studio programming languages are built around the .NET, including C#. Microsoft has integrated support for .NET in all its new programming languages and development tools, including Microsoft XNA Game Studio 3.1, giving it access to a wide range of resources and development technologies. XNA works with .NET version 2.0.

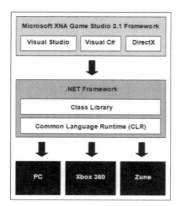

Figure 1.3
.NET 2.0 provides XNA games with access to system resources.

Hint

> The Microsoft .NET Compact Framework (.NET CF) is a specialized version of .NET designed for execution on Windows CE. It has been customized to support portable and mobile devices like mobile phones and Personal Digital Assistants (PDAs). The Zune media player utilizes a specialized version of .NET CF as does the Xbox 360. These device's version of .NET CF utilizes the same runtime as .NET CF, only these versions of .NET CF use a restricted subset of the .NET CF class library.

The .NET Framework serves as an interface between XNA and the operating system. It is responsible for translating program source code into an executable format that can run on a target operating system (computer, Xbox 360, or Zune player). Figure 1.3 illustrates .NET 2.0's roles in supporting application development.

The .NET 2.0 Framework consists of two key components, the .NET Framework class library and the common language runtime (CLR). The .NET class library is a hierarchical collection of classes that define the different types of objects that can be instantiated (created) within your games. These classes provide access to an enormous collection of prewritten code defined as part of methods. The CLR compiles XNA code statements into an executable format for a given target environment. The CLR also provides other services, including Memory Management and Exception Handling.

Computer Game Development

Microsoft XNA Game Studio 3.1 installs and runs on Windows computers, providing everything needed to support the development of Windows games and applications. In addition, XNA supports game development for Microsoft's Zune media player and its Xbox 360 game console. For individuals that sign up for Microsoft's XNA Creator's Club, Microsoft even allows you to submit your games to the Xbox Live Marketplace.

Zune

Zune is the name of a Microsoft-developed portable media player. Zune is also the name of the computer software that is installed on the PC to manage the player. The Zune is supported by Microsoft's Zune Marketplace, where Zune users can go to download more than 3,000,000 songs, videos, podcasts, games, and audio books. The Zune can also be used to store and display pictures and graphic images and to play FM radio. The Zune can connect wirelessly to other Zune players to share files. It can connect to Windows computers and the Xbox 360 via a USB cable.

The Zune comes in various sizes, models, and colors, as shown in Figure 1.4. However, all of these players share the same basic set of hardware and

Figure 1.4
Visit http://www.zune.net to learn about individual Zune models.

software. This allows each device to support the same set of services, including game play.

Zune is a primary competitor to Apple's iPod. As of the writing of this book, the Zune had total unit sales in excess of 3,000,000 players. The Zune's operating system is based on the Windows CE kernel. It uses a graphical user interface (GUI) that Microsoft calls a Twist Interface, which displays options for Music, Videos, Pictures, Social, Radio, Marketplace, Games, and Settings.

The Zune is operated and controlled through a circular touch pad that XNA games automatically map to and work with much like an Xbox 360 gamepad controller. Zune games, like those shown in Figure 1.5, are distributed via the Zune Marketplace where they can be downloaded for free. The Zune is capable of playing both standalone games and multiplayer wireless games with other Zune

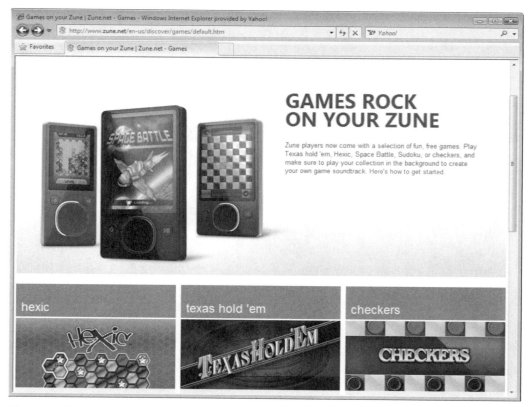

Figure 1.5
Examples of different games available for the Zune player.

players. Using XNA, you can create computer games that run on the Zune that make use of both graphics and sound.

Xbox 360

The Xbox 360 is the second video game console created by Microsoft. Its website is http://www.xbox.com. It competes with the Nintendo Wii and Sony PlayStation 3 for supremacy in the home console video game market. The Xbox 360 supports standalone, multi-player, and Internet game play (through its Xbox Live service). Xbox Live players from around the world can partner or compete head-to-head.

Xbox Live also provides access to an assortment of different types of content, including downloadable games, movies, TV shows, and demos. In addition, Xbox Live also makes games developed by members of the XNA Creators Club available for download, allowing their developers to sell them for profit. As of the writing of this book, over 30 million Xbox 360 game consoles had been sold. Considering that an estimated 70 percent of all Xbox Live users have downloaded some form of content from Xbox Live, this provides access to a considerable target market.

Microsoft allows all Xbox users to join Xbox Live for free by setting up a Silver account. With this account, users can create a custom profile, access the Xbox Live Marketplace, and communicate with other members. However, a Silver account does not allow multiplayer gaming. For this, you must purchase a Premium account, which will cost you $49.99 per year.

Getting Started with XNA 3.1

Depending on the platforms you plan to develop computer games for, you have a number of steps to perform to set up your XNA game development environment. First, you must install Microsoft Visual C# 2008 Express. This is the programming language that you will use to develop the programming logic that makes your games work. Once this has been done, you can install Microsoft XNA Game Studio 3.1. During the installation of Microsoft XNA Game Studio 3.1, XNA will automatically bind itself to Microsoft Visual C# 2008 Express.

Once you have downloaded and installed both Microsoft Visual C# 2008 Express and Microsoft XNA Game Studio 3.1, you can begin developing computer games for Microsoft Windows. If you want to develop games that run on Microsoft

Zune then you will need to purchase a Zune on which to run your games. No additional software beyond Microsoft XNA Game Studio 3.1 is required to make the connection between your personal computer and your Zune player.

If you want to create and deploy games to Microsoft Xbox 360, you will of course need an Xbox 360. In addition, you will need to join Xbox Live and download and install the XNA Game Studio Connect add-on on your Xbox 360. If you want to market your games on the Xbox Live Marketplace, you will have to sign up for the XNA Creators Club.

Downloading and Installing Microsoft Visual C# 2008 Express onto Your Computer

Before installing C#, make sure that your computer's software is up to date. To do so, click on Start > All Programs > Windows Update > Windows Update. Once this is done, you can download and install Microsoft Visual C# 2008 Express as outlined below.

Hint

All of the figures that you will see in this book are based on Windows Vista. So you may notice small differences if you are working with Windows XP or Windows 7. However, you won't see any major differences.

1. Go to http://www.microsoft.com/express/vcsharp/ as shown in Figure 1.6 and click on the Download link.

2. Click on Save when prompted to download a copy of vcssetup.exe to your computer.

3. If prompted, clicked on Continue to give Windows permission to perform the install.

4. The Welcome to Setup screen appears. Click on Next to start the installation process.

5. Select the I Have Read and Accept the License Terms option and click on Next.

6. You will then be presented with the option of installing Microsoft SQL Server 2008 Express Edition. You can install it if you want. However, you do not need it for this book or to build XNA games. Click on Next.

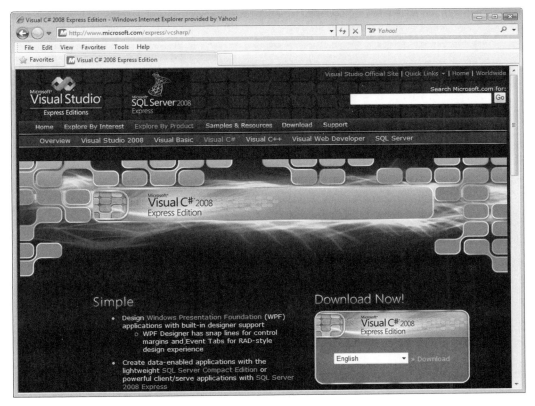

Figure 1.6
Downloading Microsoft Visual C# 2008 Express.

7. Click on Install.

8. When the installation process completes, click on Exit.

Hint

You will need to register Microsoft Visual C# 2008 Express within 30 days by clicking on Help > Register Production. Once you provide all of the required registration information, you will be presented with a 14-character registration key. Copy and paste this key into the Registration Window and click on the Complete Registration button.

Once the installation process is complete, click on Start and you will see Microsoft Visual C# 2008 Express Edition on the Start Menu. Figure 1.7 shows how Visual C# looks when first started.

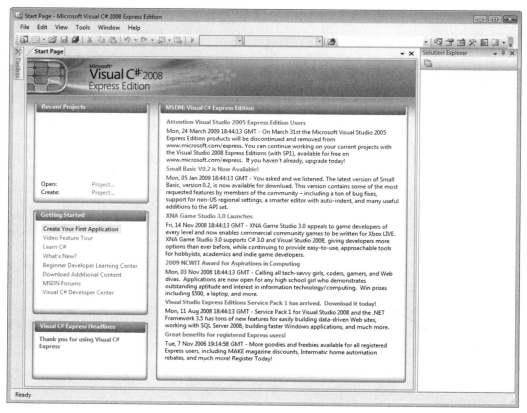

Figure 1.7
An example of how Visual C# 2008 Express looks when initially loaded on a computer running Microsoft Vista.

Installing Microsoft XNA Game Studio 3.1 onto Your Computer

Microsoft XNA Game Studio 3.1 installs like any other Windows application. The following procedure outlines the steps that are involved.

1. Go to http://creators.xna.com and click on the Resources menu and then select the Download option.

2. Click on the link to download XNA Game Studio 3.1. This will take you to the Microsoft XNA Game Studio 3.1 page where you can click on the Download button.

3. Click on Save and specify the location where you want to store the XNA's installation program. A file named XNAGS31_setup.exe will be downloaded.

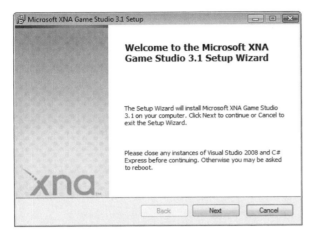

Figure 1.8
The setup wizard will guide you through the installation process.

4. Double-click on the XNA installation program. Click on Continue if prompted for permission to continue.

5. The Welcome to XNA Game Studio 3.1 Setup Wizard window appears, as shown in Figure 1.8. Click on Next.

6. The Microsoft Software License Terms are displayed. Read them and then select the I accept the terms in the License Agreement option and click on Next.

7. You will then be prompted to allow Game Studio and XNA games to communicate through the firewall on your computer as shown in Figure 1.9. Click on Yes, I Wish to Select These Rules to Enable, and then enable both of the following options and click on Install.

   ■ Allow communications between an Xbox 360 and your computer on the local subnet.
   ■ Allow the communication of network games built on the XNA Framework.

8. XNA Game Studio 3.1 will copy files to your computer and complete the installation process. Once the process is complete, a message is displayed announcing that Microsoft XNA Game Studio 3.1 was installed into Microsoft Visual C# 2008 Express. The Take Me to the XNA Creators Club Online Website option is displayed and enabled.

9. Click on Finish.

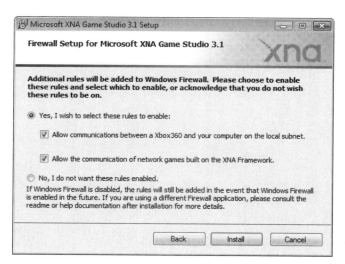

Figure 1.9
Configuring the operations of XNA.

Figure 1.10
The Microsoft XNA Game Studio 3.1 install process installs a number of components onto your computer.

Now that the Microsoft XNA Game Studio 3.1 install process is complete, you can go to Start > Microsoft XNA Game Studio 3.1 to view its components, as demonstrated in Figure 1.10.

Creating an Xbox Live Account

If you plan on creating games for the Xbox 360, you will need to set up a connection between your computer and your Xbox 360. To do so, you will have to download and install the XNA Game Studio Connect Game add-on application on your Xbox 360. Before you can do this, you must sign up with Xbox Live. Before that, you first need to sign up for a free Windows Live ID and create your game tag (if you do not already have one). The steps for doing so are outlined here.

1. On your computer, open your web browser and go to `http://creators.xna.com/` and click on Home > Membership. The Membership page is displayed.

2. Scroll down and click on the link to sign up for a free Windows Live ID. A page similar to the one shown in Figure 1.11 will be displayed.

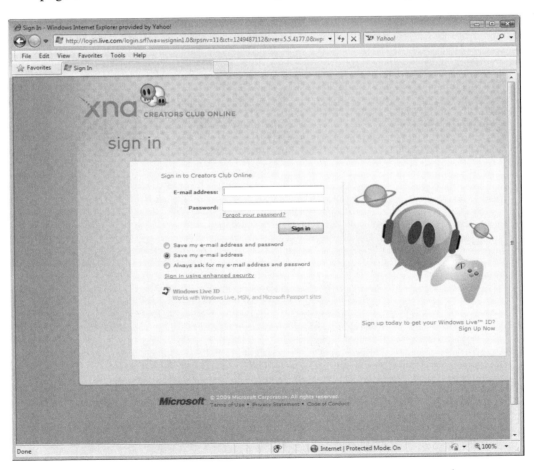

Figure 1.11
You must have a Windows Live ID to begin the process.

3. You need a Windows Live ID to begin this process. If you have one, enter the e-mail address you used to set up the account along with the password. If you do not have a Windows Live ID, click on the Sign Up Now link to create one and then continue on with the rest of this procedure when done creating your Windows Live Account.

4. When requested, enter your date of birth and the name you want to assign as your Gamertag, as shown in Figure 1.12.

5. To see if the Gamertag you supplied is available, click on the Check Availability button. If that Gamertag name has already been assigned to someone else, you will have to select a different one.

Figure 1.12
Providing the information needed to create your Gamertag.

6. Once you have supplied an available Gamertag, scroll down and select one of the following zones.

- Recreation
- Family
- Pro
- Underground

7. If you want you may sign up for an optional Xbox Insider newsletter and an optional Xbox partner deals/e-mail options.

8. Click on the I accept button.

9. Click on the Done button.

Now that you have created your windows Live ID and Gamertag, you are ready to set up your Xbox Live account. Begin by plugging in your Xbox 360 to your Internet router. When you do, your Xbox 360 will automatically connect to Microsoft's Xbox Live network. You may be prompted to upload a new Xbox Experience, which will replace your Xbox 360's menu system with a more user-friendly interface. This only takes a few minutes after which you are logged out.

Hint

Microsoft recently released a new graphical user interface for the Xbox 360 called the New Xbox Experience (NXE) which is designed to ease console navigation and introduce the use of avatars.

At this point, you can sign up for an Xbox Live account. When you do so, you will be asked to enter your e-mail address and create a password and will then be required to accept the Xbox Live terms of use and privacy statement. You will also have to supply your first and last name as well as your phone number. Xbox Live will use this information to associate your Xbox Live account with your Windows Live ID and Gamertag. When prompted, click on Done to finish creating your Xbox Live account.

Hint

The Xbox Live account that you have just created will allow you to connect to the Xbox Live Marketplace, view information about available game and movie titles, and to perform downloads. It will not, however, allow you to play online games. To do that you will have to sign up for a Premium membership, which will cost you $49.99 for a year.

Connecting Your Xbox 360 and Zune to Your Computer

The process of setting up a connection between your Xbox 360 and your computer is a 3-step process, with steps that must be performed beginning on the Xbox 360 and ending on your computer. You will only need to perform this connection setup one time. Once successfully established, you will not have to repeat this procedure again. Both your Xbox 360 and computer will store connection-setting data and automatically retrieve it for future connection sessions.

Connecting Your Xbox 360 to Your Internet Router

To get your Xbox 360 talking to your computer, you are going to need to physically connect them to the same network. You can do this by connecting your Xbox 360, via Ethernet, to your Internet router or network hub. Alternatively, you can purchase and install a wireless network adapter for your Xbox 360 if you have a wireless home network.

Setting Up a Connection with Your Computer

Once you have created your Xbox Live account, you will need to download the XNA Game Studio Connect Game add-on to download the software that your Xbox 360 will need to use to establish a connection to your personal computer. The procedure is provided here:

1. On Xbox Live, go to Game Marketplace and click on Explore Game Content.

2. Click on Browse and then scroll down to the letter X, select it, and then locate and select the XNA Creators Club.

3. Click on XNA Game Studio Connect Game add-on and confirm the download when prompted.

4. When done, click on Play Now and you will see a screen like the one depicted in Figure 1.13.

5. Write down the connection code key generated by Xbox 360 and then switch over to your computer and click on Start > XNA Game Studio Device Center. The window shown in Figure 1.14 will appear.

Figure 1.13
The process of setting up a connection between Xbox 360 and your computer is begun on your Xbox 360.

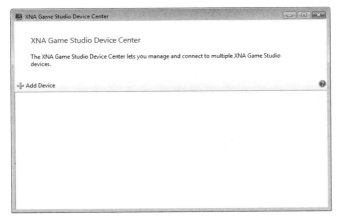

Figure 1.14
You need to add an Xbox instance to the XNA Game Studio Device Center.

6. Click on Add Device. The window shown in Figure 1.15 will appear.

7. Select Xbox 360 and type in a name for your Xbox 360, as demonstrated in Figure 1.16, and click on Next.

8. The next window that you see prompts you to enter the connection code generated by your Xbox 360, as shown in Figure 1.17. Enter the code and click on Next.

9. After a few moments a message should be displayed informing you that a successful connection has been established with your Xbox 360. Click on Finish.

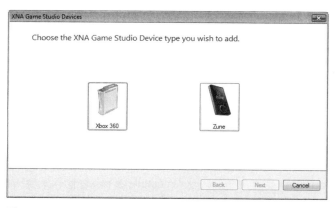

Figure 1.15
Select the Xbox 360 icon.

Figure 1.16
Enter a name for the Xbox console.

Figure 1.17
Enter the connection key generated by your Xbox 360.

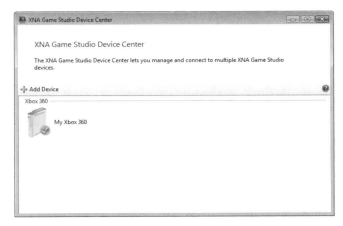

Figure 1.18
You should see an icon representing your Xbox 360 in the XNA Game Studio Device center window.

10. You should now see an Xbox 360 icon in the XNA Game Studio Devices window, as shown in Figure 1.18.

Connecting Your Zune to Your Computer

If you want to develop computer games for the Zune, you are going to need a Zune player and the Zune's USB cable. Using this cable, connect your Zune player to your computer. If you have the Zune software installed on your computer it will automatically start, allowing you to manage the Zune and to connect to the Zune Marketplace. You will need to shut down the Zune application before proceeding. When you are ready, execute the following procedure to set up a connection between your computer and the Zune player.

Hint

To manage your Zune player from your computer and to visit the Zune Marketplace, you must install the Zune software, available for free at http://www.zune.net/en-US/software/.

1. On your computer click on Start > XNA Game Studio Device Center. The XNA Game Studio Device Center window appears.

2. Click on Add Device and then select the Zune icon. A new window will appear showing a list of any Zune devices currently connected to the computer. Select your Zune player and click on Next.

3. After a few moments a message should be displayed informing you that a successful connection has been established with your Xbox 360. Click on Finish.

4. You should now see a Zune icon in the XNA Game Studio Devices window.

As with the Xbox 360, you should only have to perform this procedure one time for each Zune player you work with.

Joining the XNA Creators Club

If you want to try your hand at marketing your Xbox 360 games via Xbox Live's Marketplace, you will need to sign up for a XNA Creators Club membership, which will cost you $99. To sign up, use your Xbox 360 to go to the Xbox Live Marketplace. Click on Explore Game Content, then click on Browse, scroll down to the letter X, select it, and then select XNA Creators Club and follow the instructions provided. Any games you submit will be made available for community review and if approved will be made available for purchase and download.

Summary

This chapter provided a broad overview of Microsoft XNA Game Studio 3.1. This included a review of all the major technologies that are included in XNA game development as well as the platforms that XNA supports. You also learned how to set up your game development environment. In Chapter 2 you will build upon this knowledge by learning how to work with Visual Studio 2008 Express and will review the basic steps involved in creating an XNA game and deploying it to your computer Xbox 360 and Zune player.

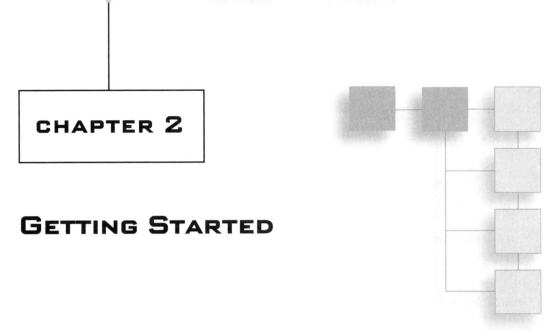

CHAPTER 2

GETTING STARTED

In this chapter, you will be introduced to the Visual Studio 2008 IDE. You will use the IDE to create your XNA games and applications and to develop the C# program code that makes them work. You will also be introduced to IDE menus and toolbars and learn about all its major windows and their features and capabilities. You will learn how to move things around in the IDE and to customize its appearance to suit your own preference. You will also learn how to work with Intellisense Everywhere and various other code editor features.

An overview of the major topics covered in this chapter includes:

- Learning about the major components that comprise the Visual Studio IDE

- Learning how to work with and control IDE menus and toolbars

- Developing an understanding of code editor features and functionality

- A review of the core set of program files generated by XNA as part of every new game

Getting to Know the Visual Studio 2008 Express IDE

In this book you will learn how to create XNA games using the Visual Studio 2008 Express IDE. The Visual Studio 2008 Express IDE provides essential tools for game development such as a compiler that translates program code into an executable program, a debugger that you can use to locate and fix problems with program code, and various tools needed to manage game projects.

The Visual Studio 2008 Express IDE features a standard menu, toolbars, and a variety of different windows. So much has been crammed into the IDE that it is not possible to display all of the IDE's toolbars and windows at the same time. Instead, Visual Studio 2008 Express allows the IDE to share space using tabbed windows and thumbnailed windows.

Figure 2.1 shows Visual Studio 2008 Express IDE when used to create and work on an XNA 3.1 game.

As Figure 2.1 shows, Visual Studio 2008 Express's IDE consists of a number of elements, which are covered in detail throughout this chapter.

One particularly handy feature of the IDE is AutoDock, which lets you move and reposition IDE windows using your mouse. When you move a window close to

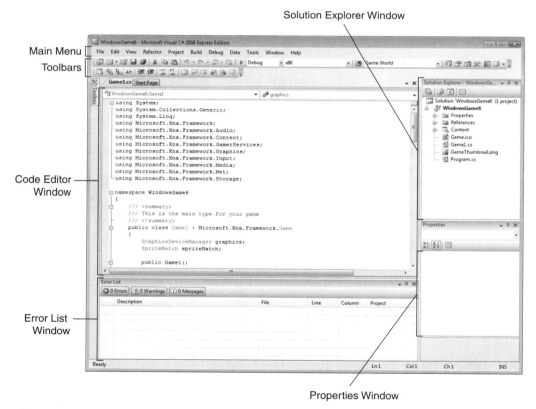

Figure 2.1
The Visual Studio 2008 Express IDE consists of multiple menus, toolbars, and windows.

the edge of the IDE, an outline is displayed that shows you where the IDE will re-dock the windows in the IDE if you let go of it. AutoDock makes it easy for you to modify windows placement within the IDE, allowing you to customize window locations to suit your preference.

You need to be careful when repositioning windows. With so many windows, it is easy to misplace, close, or accidentally move them. If you accidentally or deliberately close a window, you can always add it back by clicking on the View menu and selecting it. The IDE contains so many different windows that it cannot display them all at once under the View menu. If the window you are looking for is not listed, select the Other Windows option and look for it there.

To free up space, many of the IDE's windows are designed so that they can assume a tabbed format within a shared window space. By clicking on the appropriate tab, you can switch between windows.

Another cool feature supported by the IDE is an autohide feature that allows you to shrink a window to a tab connected to the edge of the IDE. By temporarily hiding windows, you can free up space in the IDE without having to close other windows. Later, you can restore docked windows by clicking on their tab. As an example of how the thumbtack option works, look at Figure 2.2. Here, the Solution Explorer window is docked as a tab on the right side of the IDE. This provides more room for the Properties window.

Trick

The Visual Studio 2008 Express IDE is highly customizable. To configure the display of toolbars, click on Tools > Customize. To customize code editor behavior, click on Tools > Options.

Navigating IDE Menus

The Visual Studio 2008 Express IDE includes a comprehensive collection of menu commands. Visual Studio 2008 Express manages menus dynamically. Menu availability changes based on the task being performed and the state of the project. A summary of Visual Studio 2008 Express's menus is provided here:

- **File.** Contains commands for opening and saving projects and solutions.

- **Edit.** Contains text-editing commands like Undo, Copy, Cut, and Paste as well as commands for setting bookmarks and interacting with Intellisense.

- **View.** Contains commands that let you switch between the different IDE windows as well as enable and disable IDE toolbars.

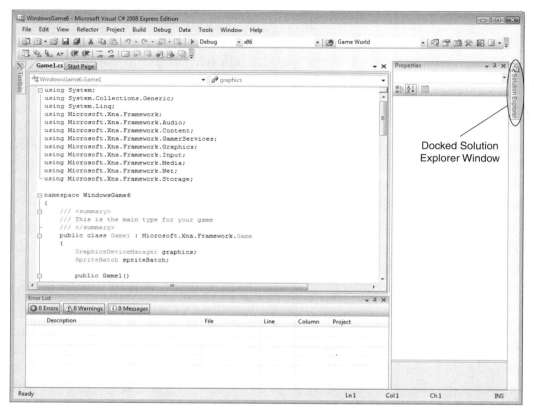

Figure 2.2
AutoDock is a quick and easy way to free up space within the Visual Studio 2008 Express IDE.

- **Refactor.** Contains advanced commands that allow you to make changes to program code.

- **Project.** Contains commands that add different resources to your game projects.

- **Build.** Contains commands that build and compile your games and package and publish your games.

- **Debug.** Contains commands that you can use to test and debug a game's execution.

- **Data.** Contains commands that let you set up connections to data sources such as a local database.

- **Tools.** Provides access to commands and windows that you can use to configure the IDE and launch the XNA Game Studio Device Center.

- **Window.** Contains commands that let you arrange and manage windows.

- **Help.** Access to Visual Studio 2008 Express help system.

Working with Toolbars

Like most Windows applications, Visual Studio 2008 Express supplies toolbars that provide single-click access to certain commands. By default, Visual Studio 2008 Express displays its Standard and Text Editing toolbars, as shown in Figure 2.3. As with menu commands, access to toolbar commands varies depending on what you are doing.

Hint

The Visual Studio 2008 Express IDE includes more than a dozen toolbars. You can configure the display of most toolbars by clicking on the View > Toolbars. In addition, you can configure all toolbars by clicking on Tools > Customize.

Visual Studio 2008 Express has too many toolbars to go over them all. However, you can learn more about toolbar commands by placing the mouse pointer over its icon. This displays the command's name/function as a ToolTip.

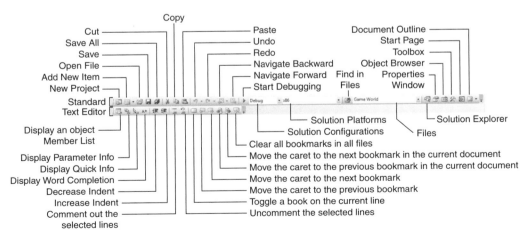

Figure 2.3
Toolbars provide access to commonly used commands and windows.

Getting to Know the Code Editor

Visual Studio 2008 Express's code editor, shown in Figure 2.4, is the window you will work with when adding and editing programming code to your XNA games. It is automatically displayed whenever you create or open a new game project.

Trick

The code editor is highly configurable. To do so, click on Tools > Options. The Options window appears. Expand the Text Editor Basic link and then select the Editor option (on the left-hand side of the Options window). You may modify any of the settings displayed on the right-hand side of the window.

Take note of the two drop-down lists located at the top of the code editor. The first drop-down list is the Class Name list which lets you select any objects located within your application. The second drop-down list lets you access any method defined within the currently selected object. Using these two drop-down lists together, you can locate any method defined within your game project.

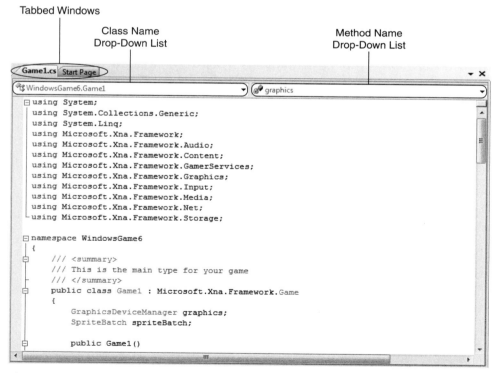

Figure 2.4
The code editor is used to add and modify program code in your XNA Games.

Pre-written Program Code

When it comes to writing the program code that makes your games work, Visual Studio helps make things simple by writing a lot of the code for you. To see what I mean, create a new project by starting Microsoft Visual C# 2008 Express and then clicking on File > New Project > Windows Game 3.1. In Response, Visual Studio 2008 Express will create a new project for you. As you will see, the following C# code statements are automatically created for you as part of your new XNA project.

```csharp
using System;
using System.Collections.Generic;
using System.Linq;
using Microsoft.Xna.Framework;
using Microsoft.Xna.Framework.Audio;
using Microsoft.Xna.Framework.Content;
using Microsoft.Xna.Framework.GamerServices;
using Microsoft.Xna.Framework.Graphics;
using Microsoft.Xna.Framework.Input;
using Microsoft.Xna.Framework.Media;
using Microsoft.Xna.Framework.Net;
using Microsoft.Xna.Framework.Storage;

namespace WindowsGame2
{
    /// <summary>
    /// This is the main type for your game
    /// </summary>
    public class Game1 : Microsoft.Xna.Framework.Game
    {
        GraphicsDeviceManager graphics;
        SpriteBatch spriteBatch;

        public Game1()
        {
            graphics = new GraphicsDeviceManager(this);
            Content.RootDirectory = "Content";
        }

        /// <summary>
        /// Allows the game to perform any initialization it needs to
        /// before starting to run. This is where it can query for any
        /// required services and load any non-graphic related content.
```

```
/// Calling base.Initialize will enumerate through any components
/// and initialize them as well.
/// </summary>
protected override void Initialize()
{
    // TODO: Add your initialization logic here

    base.Initialize();
}

/// <summary>
/// LoadContent will be called once per game and is the place to
/// load all of your content.
/// </summary>
protected override void LoadContent()
{
    // Create a new SpriteBatch, which can be used to draw textures.
    spriteBatch = new SpriteBatch(GraphicsDevice);

    // TODO: use this.Content to load your game content here
}

/// <summary>
/// UnloadContent will be called once per game and is the place to
/// unload all content.
/// </summary>
protected override void UnloadContent()
{
    // TODO: Unload any non ContentManager content here
}

/// <summary>
/// Allows the game to run logic such as updating the world,
/// checking for collisions, gathering input, and playing audio.
/// </summary>
/// <param name="gameTime">Provides a snapshot of timing
/// values.</param>
protected override void Update(GameTime gameTime)
{
    // Allows the game to exit
    if (GamePad.GetState(PlayerIndex.One).Buttons.Back ==
        ButtonState.Pressed)
        this.Exit();
```

```
        // TODO: Add your update logic here

        base.Update(gameTime);
    }

    /// <summary>
    /// This is called when the game should draw itself.
    /// </summary>
    /// <param name="gameTime">Provides a snapshot of timing
    /// values.</param>
    protected override void Draw(GameTime gameTime)
    {
        GraphicsDevice.Clear(Color.CornflowerBlue);

        // TODO: Add your drawing code here

        base.Draw(gameTime);
    }
  }
}
```

Trick

The format of the code statements you will see when creating a new XNA project will vary slightly from what you see here. To make things fit nicely onto the pages of this book, I had to split some code statements into multiple parts, spread out over two or more lines. C# recognizes when code statements are spread out over multiple lines and has no problem processing them.

These statements provide a template that outlines the overall organization of the game program code. To develop the game's programming logic, all you have to do is enter its code statements into the right locations. A detailed examination of these code statements and their purpose is provided in Chapter 3.

Color Coding, Automatic Indentation, and Spacing

The code editor automatically does a number of things that help you when entering your code statements. For example, C# keywords are color-coded. This makes them stand out. Color-coding provides visual indicators that make program code easier to read and understand. As demonstrated in Figure 2.5, the code editor also automatically indents your code statements. Indenting code statements helps visually organize code statements, making program code easier to read and understand.

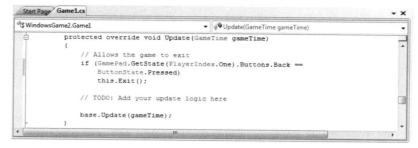

Figure 2.5
The code editor automatically color codes and indents statements.

Yet another code editor feature is automatic spacing. As an example, enter the following code statement on any blank line in the code editor.

```
bool gameOver=true;
```

Press the Enter key and watch as the code editor changes the statement to the format shown below.

```
bool gameOver = true;
```

The changes made by the editor are small but important. Notice that two blank spaces have been added (before and after the equals sign). This has made the statement easier to read by automatically handling things like color coding, indentation, and statement formatting. The code editor lets you keep your focus on the task at hand without having to sweat the small stuff.

Taking Advantage of "IntelliSense Everywhere"

Another extremely helpful code editor feature is *IntelliSense Everywhere*, which monitors you as you type and offers suggestions for completing code statements. IntelliSense Everywhere interacts with you by displaying the pop-up boxes as you type. These pop-up boxes display lists of code snippets applicable to the current state of the statement that you are keying in.

As an example of how IntelliSense Everywhere works, I have started creating a new C# statement. I have typed the letters str and paused. In response, Intellisense Everywhere has displayed a list of options for completing the current work as shown in Figure 2.6. To save time typing and eliminate the possibility of making any typos, all I had to do was select the choice that matched what I had planned on typing. To select a choice all you have to do is scroll up or down to find it and then click on it with the mouse.

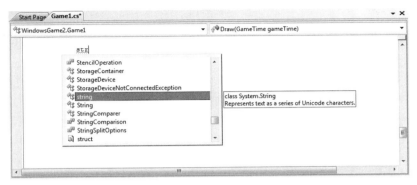

Figure 2.6
IntelliSense Everywhere helps speed up the process of writing code while reducing typos and careless mistakes.

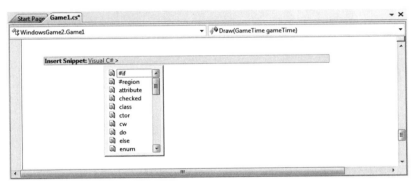

Figure 2.7
Code snippets are available for most major C# programming constructs.

Trick

You can also use the Ctrl and Space keys together to manually start Intellisense Everywhere.

Another helpful Intellisense Everywhere feature is its support for code snippets. A *code snippet* is a template statement that you can insert directly into your program code and then fill out. To instruct Visual Studio to assist you by adding a code snippet to your project, all you have to do is right-click on the location in the code editor where you want to insert the snippet and then click on the Insert Snippet option. To insert a C# snippet, you would double click on the Visual C# folder icon that is displayed. In response a list of code snippets for different C# programming constructs is displayed as demonstrated in Figure 2.7.

Once you find the snippet you need, click on it to insert it into your program code. Once inserted, you can fill in the highlighted areas in the snippet code as demonstrated in Figure 2.8.

Introducing the Solution Explorer

As demonstrated in Figure 2.9, the Solution Explorer displays all the projects and files that make up an XNA game. It organizes everything in a hierarchical format, starting with the solution, followed by the projects it contains and then the individual files that make up the projects. The following list outlines the major resource files and container shown in Figure 2.9.

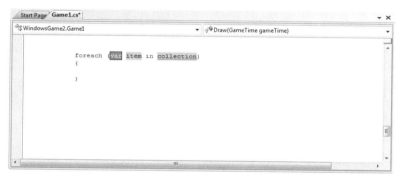

Figure 2.8
Snippets speed up code development and help eliminate syntax errors by assisting in statement formulation.

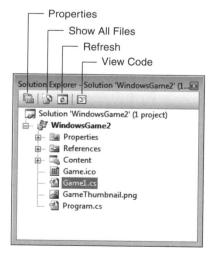

Figure 2.9
Solution Explorer lets you manage the projects and files that make up XNA games.

- **Properties.** Provides access to general application, debug, and other project resources properties.

- **References.** Contains links (references) to assemblies that are automatically added to your game projects.

- **Content.** Stores content that is automatically generated as part of your games.

- **Game.ico.** A 32 × 32 graphic icon that represents your game's executable file when displayed on Microsoft windows.

- **Game1.cs.** A code file that contains your game's programming logic.

- **GameThumbnail.png.** An icon file that is displayed as part of your game's distribution package. This icon is used to create a game thumbnail that is displayed for the game when ported to the Zune Player or Xbox 360.

- **Program.cs.** A code file generally used by game developers only in more advanced games.

Using Solution Explorer you can locate and open any file by double-clicking on it. If, for example, you select one of the files with a .cs file extension, its contents are displayed within the code editor, where you can edit and modify it as necessary.

Hint
_____

> A *solution* is a container used to store one or more projects that make up your XNA games. If you plan on writing XNA games for the PC, Xbox 360, and Zune, you will end up storing a different project for each type of application.

Understanding the Properties Window

Properties specify the values (attributes) assigned to the resources and objects that make up your XNA games. If you select one of the resources listed in the Solution Explorer window, all of its properties are displayed in the Properties window. You can view and often modify individual properties by selecting them in Solution Explorer and then typing in a new value. Figure 2.10 shows an example of properties belonging to the GameThumbnail.png file.

As shown in Figure 2.10, each property's name is displayed in the left-hand column of the Property window and its assigned value is displayed in the

Categorized
Alphabetical
Property Pages

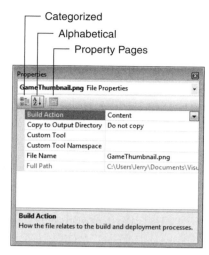

Figure 2.10
Using the Properties window to view information about project contents.

Figure 2.11
The Error List window displays a listing of errors, warnings, and messages flagged by Visual Studio.

right-hand column. By default, the property content is organized by category. If you prefer, you can sort properties alphabetically.

Working with the Error List Window

As you work on your XNA games, there will be times where mistakes are made. Your mistakes will be reported as errors and warnings in the Error List window as demonstrated in Figure 2.11.

In order to be able to compile and execute your XNA games, you must locate and eliminate all errors from your games. By keeping an eye on the Error List window, you can determine when an error is detected. To locate an error within your program code, all you have to do is double-click on the error message and the statement containing the error will be displayed in the code editor. Warnings identify situations where problems may occur. However, warnings do not prevent your games from compiling and executing. However, it is important that you eliminate all warnings from your program code as well.

If you look at the three errors listed in Figure 2.11, you will see that a lot of information has been provided to help you figure out what the problem is. The information provided includes a description of the problem, the name of the source code file where the error resides, and the line and column location where the error was detected.

Summary

This chapter introduced you to the Visual Studio 2008 IDE. You were given an overview of IDE menus and the Standard and Text Editor toolbars. You learned about all of the IDE's major windows and their features and capabilities. This included learning about the Code Editor window and its support for automatic indentation, color-coding, and Intellisense Everywhere. You learned how to move things around in the IDE and to customize its appearance. In addition to all this, you learned about the major project files that XNA automatically creates for every new XNA game. In Chapter 3 you will get to expand further on your understanding of XNA development by creating your first XNA application and then examining its source code.

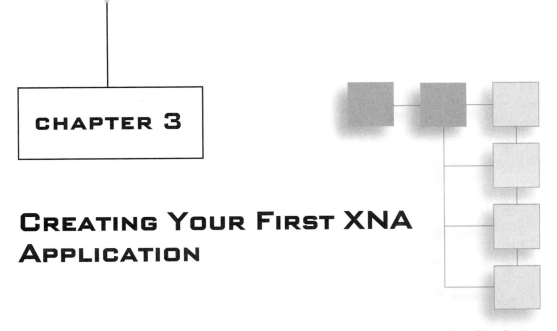

CHAPTER 3

CREATING YOUR FIRST XNA APPLICATION

In the first two chapters, you learned how the various tools and technologies come together in Microsoft XNA Game Studio 3.1 to create a complete game development environment. In Chapter 2, you were introduced to the Visual Studio IDE and learned about its major windows, toolbars, and features. In this chapter, you will learn how to create your first XNA application. This chapter will then look at the C# program code that makes the application work.

An overview of the major topics covered in this chapter includes:

- Learning how to create an XNA application for your personal computer

- Learning how to execute XNA applications

- Reviewing the basic construction of all XNA program files

Classes, Objects, Methods, and Variables

The XNA development environment is object oriented. C# is an object-oriented programming language. All of the resources used or managed by your games are viewed as objects. Objects are created based on classes. If you create a tank game, you might, for example, define all of the actions the tank can perform, like moving and firing as well as all of the attributes or properties of the tank, such as its size, color, and so forth.

The characters in your games are objects—wizards and trolls or balls and paddles or tanks. Object behavior is defined as the type of actions that object can perform or that can be performed on an object. Object behavior is defined using methods. A *method* is a collection of code statements that together perform a specific action. For example, a tank object can move, shoot, and perhaps even temporarily shield itself from oncoming enemy fire.

Similarly, the attributes or properties that describe an object are stored as variables that belong to that object. In the case of a tank, you might define properties that specify the tank's size, speed, color, and so on. A *variable* is a pointer to a location in memory where a piece of data is stored.

Creating a Simple XNA Application

To get you up and running as quickly as possible, this chapter will show you how to create your first XNA application. This application won't do much, yet you will learn a great deal from its creation. When finished, it will simply display a window with a blue background and wait for you to close it. Later, you will enhance the application by displaying a text message in the window.

The first step in creating an XNA application is to create a new project. If you have not already done so, click on Start > All Programs > Microsoft XNA Game Studio 3.1 > Microsoft Visual C# 2008 Express. Within a few moments, Visual C# starts, as shown in Figure 3.1.

Creating a New Project

To begin the development of your new application, click on File > New Project. The New Project Window opens, as shown in Figure 3.2.

Note that the New Project window is organized into parts. In the upper-left section is a list of supported project types. For this book, we'll always be working with XNA Studio 3.1. In the upper-right side of the New Project window is the templates section. To create a new XNA application you begin by selecting a template for the type of applications you want to create. A template provides a collection of resources required to create a specific type of game. The bottom portion of the New Project window is where you assign a name to your project, specifying where it should be stored. Note that by default, the Create directory for the solution option is selected. This option results in your new project and all of the resources required to make it work to be saved in their own folder located by default in your Documents\Visual Studio 2008\Projects folder.

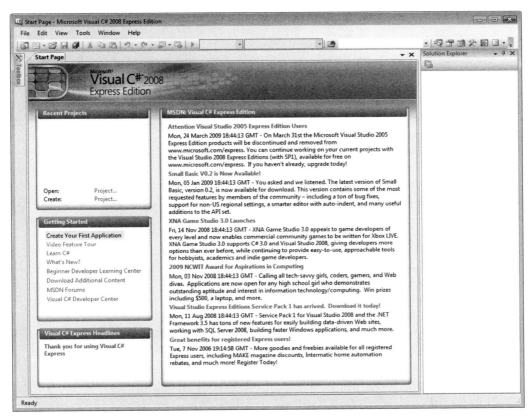

Figure 3.1
An example of how Microsoft Visual C# 2008 Express Edition looks when first started.

Hint

You can also create new XNA applications using Starter Kits. A Starter Kit is similar to a template except that it has already been highly customized to create a certain type of game. With a Starter Kit, all you have to do is tweak it a little to suit your own particular goals. As a result, Starter Kits allow you to create new games with very little effort. There are many different XNA Starter Kits available. You can download them from the Creators Club website. You can also do a quick search for the term XNA Starter Kit on the Internet.

XNA pre-installs templates for Windows, Xbox 360, and Zune games as well as for Windows, Xbox 360, and Zune libraries. For this example, select the Windows Game (3.1) template, enter MyFirstApp as the project name, and click on OK. In response, a new project is created and its contents are displayed, as shown in Figure 3.3.

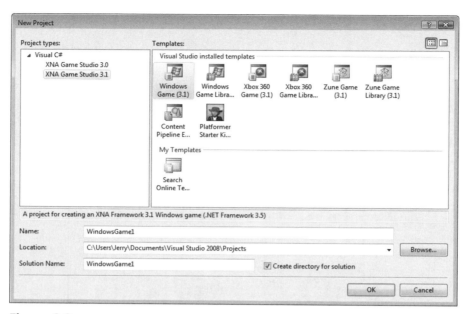

Figure 3.2
XNA Game Studio 3.1 supports the development of a host of different types of games and game libraries.

Figure 3.3 shows an example of what a new Windows Game (3.1) project looks like. Take a look at the Solution Explorer window. Note that when you created this new project, XNA Game Studio 3.1 created a new Solution named MyFirstApp. Inside the solution is a single project, also named MyFirstApp. Each project within a solution contains all of the files needed to create a new application. A brief overview of all of the files found in this project was provided in Chapter 2.

Later, when you learn how to create versions of your applications for the Zune player or Xbox 360, you will learn how to add additional projects to your solutions (one per target platform).

Hint

A *game* is a standalone application that you can run and play. A *game library* is a collection of files that serve a specific purpose and can be used in the creation of games.

Executing Your New Application

Since this is a Windows program, you can run it on the computer you used to create it. To do so, click on Debug > Start Debugging or click on the Start

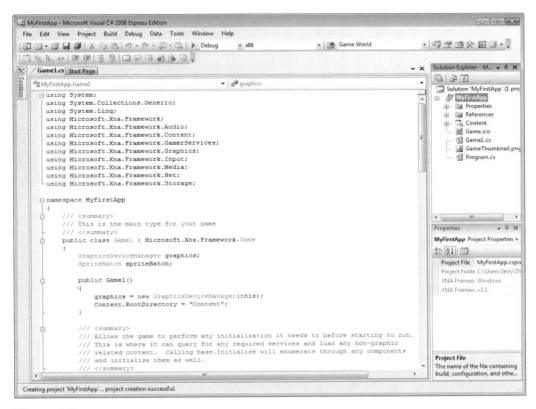

Figure 3.3
The contents of the new project will vary based on the type of template you selected.

Debugging button located on the Standard toolbar. In response, XNA Game Studio 3.1 will compile your new application (as long as it does not contain any errors) into a format that can be executed on your computer. Once a compiled version of your application has been generated, XNA runs it. Within a moment, you should see the application's window appear, as shown in Figure 3.4.

As you can see, the application's name is displayed in the Window's titlebar. To the left of the application name is an icon representing the application. You can click on it to display a context menu, as demonstrated in Figure 3.5. Minimize, Maximize, and Close buttons are also provided in the window's upper-right corner.

Figure 3.4
The application's window looks like any other Windows application.

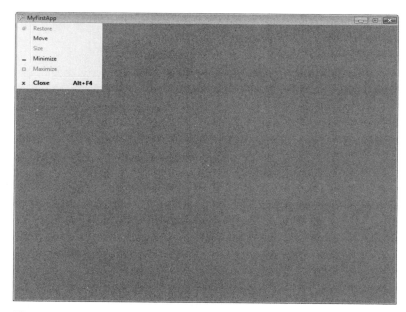

Figure 3.5
Accessing the application window's Context menu.

Hint

If you run into problems when working on an XNA project and are having trouble figuring out what's not working, you can turn to the XNA community forums page located at http://forums.xna.com/forums/ for help from your fellow game developers. These forums provide you with a means of posting questions and getting answers and help from others who have experienced the same types of problems and challenges you are facing.

Halting Application Execution

Since this application is a Windows application, you can stop it by clicking on its Close button or by displaying its context menu and then selecting the Close option. If your computer has a Microsoft Xbox 360 Gamepad controller connected to it, you can also close the application by pressing on the Gamepad's Back button.

Hint

You heard correctly; you can connect a wired Xbox 360 Gamepad to your Windows XP or Vista computer and your computer will automatically detect and install the software driver needed to work with it. Pretty cool!

In the event that your application misbehaves and won't close using any of the above options, you can return to the Visual Studio IDE and click on Debug > Stop Debugging to terminate the application's execution. This option is not recommended, since it prevents your application from terminating cleanly and closing any files or resources that it may be working with.

Examining Program Organization and Structure

Okay, I admit that the previous application is not exactly the most fun or interesting XNA application in the world. All it does is display a window with a blue background. Still, by creating this application, you have just learned the basic mechanics involved in the creation of any XNA game.

To gain an even deeper appreciation of what you have just created, let's look under the hood at the program code that makes this application run. Every time you create a new XNA project, two C# programs named Program.cs and Game1.cs are automatically created for you. If you look at the Solution Explorer window, you will see both of these programs listed.

Examining the Program.cs Program

The contents of Game1.cs should be visible, by default, in the code editor. This is the program file in your application where you will make modifications and add code of your own in order to create your own unique applications. To view the contents of Program.cs, double-click on it in Solution Explorer. When you do, the file opens and its contents are displayed in a new tab in the code editor. The code statements in this file are shown below.

```
using System;

namespace MyFirstApp
{
    static class Program
    {
        /// <summary>
        /// The main entry point for the application.
        /// </summary>
        static void Main(string[] args)
        {
            using (Game1 game = new Game1())
            {
                game.Run();
            }
        }
    }
}
```

Program.cs is the main program or the startup program for a project. When called upon for execution, it creates a new object of type Game1 and then executes its run method. This starts the execution of your game. Ordinarily, unless you are working on a very advanced game, you will not have to make any changes to this C# program.

Hint

In C# every code statement is executed within a method. A method is a collection of statements that performs a specific task.

Examining the Game1.cs Program

C# is a highly structured programming language. The programming statements that make up the Game1.cs program are organized into a very specific format, as outlined in Figure 3.6.

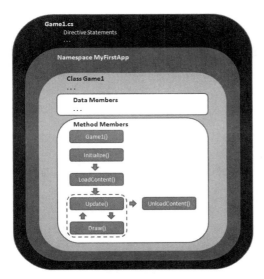

Figure 3.6
A graphical depiction of the basic structure of the Game1.cs program.

Using Directive Statements to Reference Namespaces

As Figure 3.6 shows, the Game1.cs program begins by executing declarative statements that set up references to a number of namespaces. A *namespace* is a mechanism used to categorize and group related resources. The XNA Framework organizes resources into a whole series of namespaces. By referencing a namespace, you make its resources available to your application to run. These resources include various system and .NET Framework resources. If you look closely at these statements, you see where the resources required to support things like audio, graphics, and input are included.

Defining a Local Namespace and Class

The Game1.cs defines its own namespace, named after the project name you supplied when creating the project. This namespace contains a class named Game1. A *class* is a container for groups of methods and variables that work together to define all of the features and capabilities of an object. If you want, you can add additional classes. Classes are used to store data members and method members. Data members are variables that are used to store values collected during program execution.

Defining with Data Members

Data members can be declared outside of data methods, creating class-level variables, which are accessible throughout the entire program. A couple class-level variables are defined by default. Data members declared within data methods are available only within the methods where they are defined.

Examining Method Members

As shown in Figure 3.6, a total of six methods are provided as part of every new Game1.cs program. The Game1() method is a constructor. It receives control when a new instance of the Game1 class is created. The Initialize() method is executed as soon as the program is executed. It gives you a place to initialize variables and to declare objects belonging to the Game1 object.

Once the Initialize() method finishes executing, the LoadContent() method is executed. It is also called whenever graphics content within the game is reloaded. This method is where you will load game graphics and any other content needed by your game like sound and graphic files. Once the LoadContent() method finishes executing, the game enters into its game loop. The game loop consists of two methods, Update() and Draw(), which are executing repeatedly for as long as the game runs. The Update() method is where you will define the overall controlling logic that makes your game run. Here you will write the programming logic required to interact with the player via the gamepad, mouse, or keyboard. Using the player's input, you will update the game's state, keeping track of where things are, when they collide, when points are scored, and so on.

Hint

The *game loop* is a series of code statements that repeatedly execute for as long as a game runs. A game loop is the key controlling mechanism within your XNA game. The game loop is responsible for repeatedly checking for player input, updating game state, playing music and sound effects, and displaying the game.

The Draw() method is where you will place the code statements responsible for updating the display of the game content. As a rule of thumb, you will want to restrict the program code placed in the Draw() method to just those code statements that actually update the screen display. Game play continues until the Update() method decides it should halt. Game play may be halted because the player runs out of lives or because the player presses a gamepad button or keyboard key indicating that it should stop. This stops the execution of the game loop and triggers the execution of the UnloadContent() method, which gives you a place to add any cleanup programming logic. For example, you might need to save the player's score, display game credits, or simply thank the player for playing the game. Once the UnloadContent() method finishes, the game ends.

Dissecting the Game1.cs Program

Okay, now that you have reviewed the overall organization and structure of the Game1.cs program, let's dissect the Game1.cs program that was created when you created the MyFirstApp application. To view it, all you have to do is click on its tab in the code editor. If it is not open, then you can view it by double-clicking on its entry in the Solution Explorer window. This file begins with the following directive statements.

```
using System;
using System.Collections.Generic;
using System.Linq;
using Microsoft.Xna.Framework;
using Microsoft.Xna.Framework.Audio;
using Microsoft.Xna.Framework.Content;
using Microsoft.Xna.Framework.GamerServices;
using Microsoft.Xna.Framework.Graphics;
using Microsoft.Xna.Framework.Input;
using Microsoft.Xna.Framework.Media;
using Microsoft.Xna.Framework.Net;
using Microsoft.Xna.Framework.Storage;
```

These statements make various resources available that are required for your application to run. These resources include different system and .NET Framework resources. If you look closely at these statements, you see where the resources required to support things like audio, graphics, and input are included.

Next, the application defines a local namespace as shown here.

```
namespace MyFirstApp
{
}
```

This name serves as a container for all of the remaining program statements in your application. In C# programs, program code is organized into methods. A method is a collection of statements that together perform a specific task. Methods can only exist within classes. So the next part of the Game1.cs program, shown below in bold, are the statements that define the Game1 class.

```
namespace MyFirstApp
{
    /// <summary>
    /// This is the main type for your game
    /// </summary>
    public class Game1 : Microsoft.Xna.Framework.Game
    {
        GraphicsDeviceManager graphics;
        SpriteBatch spriteBatch;
    }
}
```

As you can see, the Game1 class resides within the MyFirstApp namespace. Note that two class-level variables have already been defined for you. The GraphicsDeviceManager is an object variable based on the graphics class, which provides access to the computer's graphics device (e.g., its *graphics processing unit* or *GPU*). SpriteBatch is an object variable based on the spriteBatch class, which provides you with access to methods that you will use when updating the screen display.

Hint

> Statements that begin with the /// characters are comments. Their purpose is to document what is going on within the program code. Other than that, they are ignored by the C# compiler when the program is compiled into an executable format.

The rest of the statements in the Game1 class consist of collections of comments, statements, and methods. The first of these sets of statements, shown below, defines the Game1() method.

```
public Game1()
{
    graphics = new GraphicsDeviceManager(this);
    Content.RootDirectory = "Content";
}
```

This method is a constructor. It automatically gets control when a new instance of the Game1 class is created. As you can see, it contains two statements. The first statement defines an object variable named graphics based on the current instance of GraphicsDeviceManager. The second statement tells the program where to look for any content (e.g., graphic, audio files, and so on needed by the program). Note the reference to Content. If you look at the Solution Explorer window, you'll see this resource listed.

Next, the `Initialize()` method is defined. Take note of the embedded `TODO` comment, which identifies the location where you should add your own code, in the event you need to perform any initialization activities like setting play scores to zero or resetting the screen to its default starting view.

```
/// <summary>
/// Allows the game to perform any initialization it needs
/// before starting to run. This is where it can query for any
/// required services and load any non-graphic related content.
/// Calling base.Initialize will enumerate through any components
/// and initialize them as well.
/// </summary>
protected override void Initialize()
{
    // TODO: Add your initialization logic here

    base.Initialize();
}
```

Next the `LoadContent()` method is defined. It includes a statement that initializes a new variable object named `spriteBatch`. This method is where you will load game graphics and any other content needed by your game, like sound and graphic files. Note the inclusion of the `TODO` comment, showing where you should add any code statements of your own.

```
/// <summary>
/// LoadContent will be called once per game and is the place to
/// load all of your content.
/// </summary>
protected override void LoadContent()
{
    // Create a new SpriteBatch, which can be used to draw
    // textures.
    spriteBatch = new SpriteBatch(GraphicsDevice);

    // TODO: use this.Content to load your game content here
}
```

Next, the `UnloadContent()` method is defined. At present it does not have any actions defined. Again, take note of the inclusion of the `TODO` comment, showing where you should add any code statements of your own.

```
/// <summary>
/// UnloadContent will be called once per game and is the place
```

```
/// to unload all content.
/// </summary>
protected override void UnloadContent()
{
    // TODO: Unload any non ContentManager content here
}
```

Next, the Update() method is defined. This method is pre-supplied with a couple of code statements that merit a little extra attention. These statements, highlighted below, use the GamePad class's GetState() method to retrieve the state of a gamepad controller. Once the GamePad's state is retrieved, a check is made to determine whether the back button is being pressed. If this is the case, the player is signaling that he wishes to terminate the application and the Game class's Exit() method is executed, ending the game.

Again, you should take note of the inclusion of the TODO comment, showing where you should add any code statements of your own.

```
/// <summary>
/// Allows the game to run logic such as updating the world,
/// checking for collisions, gathering input, and playing audio.
/// </summary>
/// <param name="gameTime">Provides a snapshot of timing
/// values.</param>
protected override void Update(GameTime gameTime)
{
    // Allows the game to exit
    if (GamePad.GetState(PlayerIndex.One).Buttons.Back ==
      ButtonState.Pressed)
        this.Exit();

    // TODO: Add your update logic here

    base.Update(gameTime);
}
```

The last method to be defined is the Draw() method. This method is responsible for updating the display of the screen during game play. In its current state, this method uses the GraphicsDevice class's Clear() method to clear the screen and then redraw it using a lovely shade of Cornflower Blue.

```
/// <summary>
/// This is called when the game should draw itself.
/// </summary>
/// <param name="gameTime">Provides a snapshot of timing
```

```
/// values.</param>
protected override void Draw(GameTime gameTime)
{
    GraphicsDevice.Clear(Color.CornflowerBlue);

    // TODO: Add your drawing code here

    base.Draw(gameTime);
}
```

All this, in a nutshell, is what the Game1.cs program is set up to do when your program is initially created. As you can see, it provides you with a well-organized and solid structure into which you can then add your own programming logic, thereby creating your own custom XNA game.

Hint

The Color object supports a wide range of color properties, each of which can be specified using its property name. Table 3.1 provides a list of those properties.

Table 3.1 C# Colors

AliceBlue	AntiqueWhite	Aqua
Aquamarine	Azure	Beige
Bisque	Black	BlanchedAlmond
Blue	BlueViolet	Brown
BurlyWood	CadetBlue	Chartreuse
Chocolate	Coral	CornflowerBlue
Cornsilk	Crimson	Cyan
DarkBlue	DarkCyan	DarkGoldenrod
DarkGray	DarkGreen	DarkKhaki
DarkMagenta	DarkOliveGreen	DarkOrange
DarkOrchid	DarkRed	DarkSalmon
DarkSeaGreen	DarkSlateBlue	DarkSlateGray
DarkTurquoise	DarkViolet	DeepPink
DeepSkyBlue	DimGray	DodgerBlue
Firebrick	FloralWhite	ForestGreen
Fuchsia	Gainsboro	GhostWhite
Gold	Goldenrod	Gray
Green	GreenYellow	Honeydew

(Continued)

Table 3.1 C# Colors (*Continued*)

HotPink	IndianRed	Indigo
Ivory	Khaki	Lavender
LavenderBlush	LawnGreen	LemonChiffon
LightBlue	LightCoral	LightCyan
LightGoldenrodYellow	LightGray	LightGreen
LightPink	LightSalmon	LightSeaGreen
LightSkyBlue	LightSlateGray	LightSteelBlue
LightYellow	Lime	LimeGreen
Linen	Magenta	Maroon
MediumAquamarine	MediumBlue	MediumOrchid
MediumPurple	MediumSeaGreen	MediumSlateBlue
MediumSpringGreen	MediumTurquoise	MediumVioletRed
MidnightBlue	MintCream	MistyRose
Moccasin	NavajoWhite	Navy
OldLace	Olive	OliveDrab
Orange	OrangeRed	Orchid
PaleGoldenrod	PaleGreen	PaleTurquoise
PaleVioletRed	PapayaWhip	PeachPuff
Peru	Pink	Plum
PowderBlue	Purple	Red
RosyBrown	RoyalBlue	SaddleBrown
Salmon	SandyBrown	SeaGreen
SeaShell	Sienna	Silver
SkyBlue	SlateBlue	SlateGray
Snow	SpringGreen	SteelBlue
Tan	Teal	Thistle
Tomato	Transparent	Turquoise
Violet	Wheat	White
WhiteSmoke	Yellow	YellowGreen

Summary

This chapter has provided an overview of the essential components of all XNA games. You reviewed the basic components that make up games and drilled down into the source code to look at the organization and structure of a game's C# program code. You also learned how to create, execute, and stop your first XNA application, and in doing so, you learned the basic mechanics involved in creating and running XNA applications.

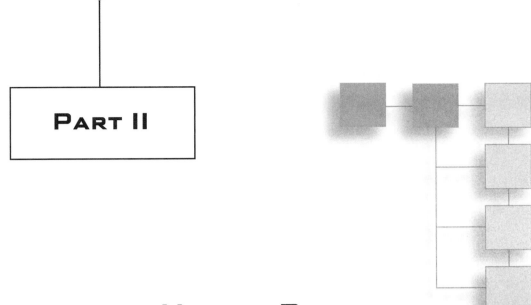

PART II

LEARNING HOW TO PROGRAM WITH VISUAL C# STUDIO EXPRESS 2008

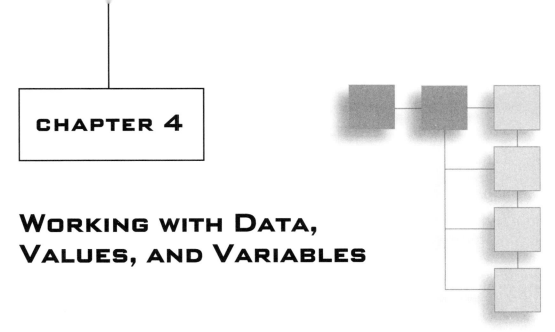

CHAPTER 4

WORKING WITH DATA, VALUES, AND VARIABLES

In order to create an XNA application that does something other than display a blue screen, you need to provide your XNA projects with a bit of program code outlining the logic that controls application activity. The language of choice is Microsoft Visual C# 2008 Express. Using C#, you can develop computer games of various levels of complexity, from very simple word games to the most complex and challenging video games. In this chapter you will learn basic C# syntax and how to document your programs with comments. In addition, you will learn a number of different ways to store individual and collections of data.

An overview of the major topics covered in this chapter includes:

- An examination of the different types of data supported by C#

- How to store data using constants, variables, and arrays

- How to perform mathematical operations and comparisons

- A review of C# reserved words

Introducing C#

Microsoft Visual C# 2008 Express is a highly structured programming language. It consists of code statements, operators, and language keywords. Programming statements end with a semicolon character (;), as demonstrated here.

```
int playerScore = 0;
```

Hint

Going forward, this book will simply use the term C# when referring to Microsoft Visual C# 2008 Express.

The semicolon character tells the C# compiler where statements end. Omit it and your game will generate errors. C# is a case-sensitive programming language. If you, for example, create and assign a variable a name of playerScore, then you must refer to it using exactly that same case. If you refer to it using any other case, such as playerscore, PLAYERSCORE, or PlayerScore, C# won't know what you are talking about.

Hint

A *variable* is a pointer to allocation in memory where data is stored. You will learn more about variables later in this chapter.

C# statements can be written on a single line or spread out over multiple lines. When writing C# code, you are free to make liberal use of white space in between code statements or to indent them in order to produce program files that are easier to look at and understand.

Hint

Because C# is case-sensitive, it is a good idea to implement a naming strategy for all the variables and methods in your programs. For example, you might consider starting all variable names with a lowercase letter and then capitalizing the first letter of each descriptive work that makes up your variables names (i.e., playerOneScore).

C# Programs Are Compiled

C# programs allow you to develop games and applications of all types. C# is a compiled programming language, which means that when you are done with an XNA project, you must compile it into an executable application that can run on its own. Just double-click on it and off it goes.

C# Is an Object-Oriented Programming Language

C# is an object-oriented programming language. It sees everything that it works with as an object. The objects are generated from classes provided by XNA or can be created from scratch using C# program code. To C#, numbers, text, and all of the other things that make up games and applications are all different types of objects. All objects have properties. *Properties* describe attributes about the object. For example, in a game of *Pong*, the ball and the paddles are objects. They have a specific size and color. By changing their properties, you can make them look different.

Objects also have methods. *A method* is a collection of statements that when executed either make an object perform a task or perform an action on the object. For example, in a *Pong* game the paddle can be made to move up and down. Similarly, the ball can be made to move around the screen and to deflect or bounce off anything it collides with (e.g., the wall or a paddle).

Documenting Your Program Code

As a game developer, you are going to end up creating a great deal of program code. In order to help make your code easier to understand and maintain, you need to embed plenty of comments in your program code. This way you can document what is going on in your program code. Comments are ignored by the C# compiler and therefore have no effect on the performance of your XNA games. For that reason, you should make liberal use of them. C# supports different types of comments, including single-line and multiline comments. To add a single-line comment, type // followed by the text that makes up the comment, as demonstrated here:

```
//This statement declares a variable named playerScore
int playerScore = 0;
```

C# is quite flexible in its support for comments, even allowing you to append them to the end of code statements, as demonstrated here:

```
int playerScore = 0; //This statement declares a variable named playerScore
```

To create multiline comments, enclose text inside the opening /* and closing */ characters, as demonstrated here:

```
/*This statement declares a variable named playerScore*/
int playerScore = 0;
```

Hint

C# also supports a third way of creating comments to facilitate the display of program documentation in an external web page. This form of comment is not used in this book. However, you will see it used in the source code generated on your behalf by XNA. Document comments are preceded by three forward slashes. As an example, look at the document comments that always precede the `Initialize()` method.

```
/// <summary>
/// Allows the game to perform any initialization it needs to before
/// starting to run. This is where it can query for any required
/// services and load any non-graphic related content. Calling
/// base.Initialize will enumerate through any components and initialize
/// them as well.
/// </summary>
protected override void Initialize()
{
    // TODO: Add your initialization logic here

    base.Initialize();
}
```

Working with Different Types of Values

C# is capable of working with many different types of values. C# uses a value's assigned data type to determine what type of operations can be performed on it. For example, numeric type values can be added, subtracted, and multiplied, whereas text variables can be concatenated and manipulated using various string methods. Table 4.1 provides a listing of different types of values that are supported by C#.

Storing and Retrieving Game Data

C# lets you work with different types of data and manage data on an individual basis or in collections. Data may be hardcoded into program code. However, more often it is collected and processed during game play. For example, an Xbox 360 game must constantly collect and process player input collected via gamepads. Windows games may have to collect and process keyboard, mouse, or gamepad data and Zune games may have to collect user input via its touchpad. C# supports a number of different ways to store data. Each option is best suited for particular situations. The best option for storing data depends on the manner in which the data is used.

- **Variables.** Used to define individual pieces of data whose value may change during game execution.

Table 4.1 C# Values

Data Type	Storage Requirements (in Bytes)	Value Range
bool	2	True or False
byte	1	0 to 255
char	2	0 to 65535
date	8	January 1, 0001 to December 31, 9999
decimal	16	0 to +/- 79,228,162,514,264,337,593,543,950,335
double	8	-1.79769313486232e308 to 1.79769313486232e308
float	4	Defines floating point numbers
int	4	-2,147,483,648 to 2,147,483,647
long	8	-9,223,372,036,854,775,808 to 9,223,372,036,854,775,807
object	4	Any type of variable
sbyte	1	-128 to 127
short	2	-32,768 to 32,767
string	Varies	Up to two billion characters
uint	4	0 to 4,294,967,295
ulong	8	0 to 18,446,744,073,709,551,615
ushort	2	0 to 65,535

- **Constants.** Used to store data that is known at design time and does not change during the game's execution. For example, a constant would be well suited for storing the mathematical constant of pi.

- **Arrays.** An index list used to store collections of related data, such as a list of names, which need to be processed and managed as a unit.

Trick

As discussed in Chapter 5, another means of storing data is to define custom classes.

Defining C# Variables

When collecting and manipulating data in your XNA games, you often need to store and retrieve that data for later use. To store individual pieces of data, you need to learn how to work with variables. A *variable* is a pointer or reference to a location within the computer's memory where the data is stored.

Before you can use a variable, you must declare it. This is done by specifying the variable's data type followed by the name you want to assign, as demonstrated here:

```
int playerAge;
```

Here, a variable named `playerAge` is declared. The variable is set up to store integer data. An integer is a numeric value that does not include any fractional data. Integers can be used to store numbers as large as 2,147,483,647, making it a good choice for storing player score in most games.

Similarly, the following example defines a variable named `playerName`, assigning it a data type of string.

```
string playerName;
```

C# lets you declare more than one variable at a time as long as they have the same data type, as demonstrated here:

```
double temp, price, miles;
```

Here three variables of type `double` are defined. Note that when declaring more than one variable at a time, each variable must be separated by a comma. Once defined, you can assign values to variables, as demonstrated here:

```
double temp, price, miles;
temp = 77.7;
price = 99.95;
miles = 30.5;
```

Here three variables of type `float` are defined and assigned values. Note that when declaring more than one variable at a time, each variable must be separated by a comma. As shown here, the equals (=) sign is an assignment operator. It takes the value specified on the right-hand side of the = sign and assigns it to the specified variable name located on the left-hand side of the = sign.

You do not have to declare a variable and then assign its initial value using two separate statements. Instead, you can accomplish everything using a single statement, as shown here:

```
double temp = 77.7, price = 99.95, miles = 30.5;
```

When you assign data to a variable that has been assigned one of C#'s many numeric-based data types, you simply assign the data followed by a semicolon. However, when assigning a value to a variable with a data type of `string`, you must enclose the value within matching quotation marks, as demonstrated here:

```
string playerName = "Alexander";
```

Naming Variables

It is important that you assign descriptive names to all your variables that identify their purpose and use. For example, a variable named x is not descriptive. A variable named player1Score, on the other hand, is quite descriptive. When formulating your variable names, you must make sure that you obey the following rules.

- Variable names can consist of letters, numbers, and the underscore character.

- The first character in a variable name must be a letter or the underscore character.

- Variable names cannot contain blank spaces.

- Variable names cannot consist of C# keywords.

To ensure that you have a good understanding of C# variable naming rules, check out Table 4.2, which provides examples of valid and invalid variable names.

C# variable names are case-sensitive. This means that you must be careful not to change the capitalization of any letters. If, for example, you declare a variable named playerScore, you must use the exact same case whenever you refer to this variable in your game's program code. If you accidently type the variable name as playerscore or playerSCORE, C# will regard these instances as references to different variables.

Table 4.2 Variable Name Examples

Variable	Description
totalScore	Valid
total_score	Valid
acct_999	Valid
email@address	Invalid (Includes an illegal character - @)
uint	Invalid (Consists of a C# keyword)
9daystogo	Invalid (Begins with a number)

Variable Scope

Depending on where you define your variables within your C# program code, they may or may not be accessible to all program statements. The term *variable scope* refers to the location in a program where a variable can be accessed. C# supports both global and local scope. A global variable is one that is accessible throughout a program, whereas a local variable is accessible only within the method where it was declared.

To define a global variable, you place its declaration statement at the beginning of the class code block, outside of any methods, as demonstrated here in bold:

```
public class Game1 : Microsoft.Xna.Framework.Game
{
    GraphicsDeviceManager graphics;
    SpriteBatch spriteBatch;
    SpriteFont font;
    String MsgText;
}
```

Here you can see a copy of the Game1 class that XNA automatically generates for you. Not shown, for the sake of brevity, are the six methods that are also part of this class. The first two variables are generated by default. The second two variables have been added, declaring a variable named font based on the SpriteFont class and a variable named MsgText based on the String class. All four of these variables are global in scope, allowing them to be accessed and modified from anywhere within the program file.

To define a local variable, you place its declaration within a method, as demonstrated here in bold:

```
protected override void Update(GameTime gameTime)
{
    // Allows the game to exit
    if (GamePad.GetState(PlayerIndex.One).Buttons.Back ==
      ButtonState.Pressed)
        this.Exit();

    SpriteFont font;
    String MsgText;

    base.Update(gameTime);
}
```

Here, two variables named `font` and `MsgText` have been defined within the `Update()` method. As such, they can only be referenced by program statements located within that method.

Storing Data That Does Not Change

If you have data that will be used by your game whose value you know will not change during game play, you should define it as a constant. This will allow C# to more efficiently store and process it. A *constant* is a value that is known at design time and does not change during game play. A constant is declared using the `const` keyword and the following syntax.

```
const type name = value
```

Here, *type* specifies the data type of the value, *name* specifies the name assigned to the constant, and *value* represents the value assigned to the constant. As the syntax shows, you must assign a constant's value as part of its declaration. This differs from variable declaration where assignment during declaration is optional. For example, the following statement defines a constant named `minValue` as an integer, assigning it a value of 0.

```
const int minValue = 0;
```

If you want, you can declare multiple constants at the same time, as demonstrated here:

```
const int MinValue = 0, MaxValue = 100;
```

Managing Collections of Data

Depending on the amount of data that your game needs to be able to work with at any one time, it may not always be practical to store data in individual variables. In these situations, you can set up arrays to store and manage large amounts of data. An *array* is an indexed list of values of like type. You can use an array to store any type of data supported by C#. To use an array, you must first define it, using the following syntax.

```
DataType[] arrayname;
```

Here, `DataType` represents the type of data that you will store in the array. The two square brackets tell C# that you are defining an array. `arrayname` is simply the name by which you will refer to the array. For example, the following statement defines an array named SuperPowers, which is capable of storing three items.

```
string[] SuperPowers = new string[3];
```

C# arrays are zero based, meaning that the first items stored in them begins at index location 0. Therefore, in the example above, data can be stored in index positions 0, 1, and 2. If an attempt is made to store data in an index position higher than 2, an error will occur.

Once defined, you can populate an array with data. To do so, you specify the name of the array, followed immediately by a pair of square brackets, the equals sign, and then the data as demonstrated here:

```
SuperPowers[0] = "Flight";
SuperPowers[1] = "Super Strength";
SuperPowers[2] = "Invisibility";
```

Accessing Array Contents

Once populated with data, you can retrieve data items from an array by specifying the index position of the item to be retrieved. For example, look at the following statements.

```
String MsgText;
string[] SuperPowers = new string[3];

SuperPowers[0] = "Flight";
SuperPowers[1] = "Super Strength";
SuperPowers[2] = "Invisibility";

MsgText = SuperPowers[2];
```

Here, a variable named MsgText is declared and an array named SuperPowers is declared. Next, three assignment statements are executed, filling the array. Lastly, the value stored in the last index position in the array is assigned to the MsgText variable. Remember, C# arrays begin at index position 0 so the third item in the array is located at index position 2 (e.g., Invisibility).

Using a Loop to Process an Array

Processing an array an element at a time can be time consuming, especially in a situation where the array may be very large, containing hundreds or thousands of items. A more efficient way of processing the contents of large arrays is using a loop, as demonstrated here:

```
String MsgText;
string[] SuperPowers = new string[3];
SuperPowers[0] = "Flight";
SuperPowers[1] = "Super Strength";
SuperPowers[2] = "Invisibility";

foreach (string power in SuperPowers)
{
    MsgText = power;
    //Do something with MstText
}
```

In this example, an array named SuperPowers has been defined and populated with three strings. A foreach loop is then used to process the contents of the array, starting at SuperPowers[0]. Each time the loop iterates, the value of power, which is a variable declared within the loop, is automatically populated with the next item stored in the loop. The value stored in power is then assigned to MsgText. The loop iterates once for each items in the array, terminating once the entire array has been processed.

Hint

A loop is a collection of programming statements that are repeatedly processed. Loops are good at processing large amounts of data or for performing repetitive tasks. You will learn all about loops in Chapter 5.

Creating Dense Arrays

If all you need is a small array to hold a limited number of values, you can define an array and populate it at the same time using a dense array, as demonstrated here:

```
int[] ExamScores = {88, 95, 70, 100, 53};
```

Note that the data used to populate the array is provided in a comma-separated list that is enclosed within a pair of matching brackets. This array is functionally equal to the following array.

```
int[] ExamScores = new int[4];
```

```
ExamScores[0] = 88;
ExamScores[1] = 95;
ExamScores[2] = 70;
ExamScores[3] = 100;
ExamScores[0] = 53;
```

Manipulating Data

Of course, there is more to working with data than simply storing and retrieving it. In most cases, your programs will have to analyze the data and process it in some manner. In order to do this, you must learn to work with mathematic, assignment, and comparison operators.

Performing Calculations

C# supports a wide range of arithmetic operators that you can use to perform virtually any type of arithmetic calculations when processing numeric data. Table 4.3 outlines these operators.

Hopefully the first four operators are familiar. However, the rest require some additional explanation. The % operator is used to divide one number within another number, returning the remainder. The x++ and ++x operators allow you to increment a numeric value by 1. The difference between these operators is the time of the update. Suppose, for example, you had two variables named playerScore and bonusLives. If bonusLives were set to 0 when the following

Table 4.3 C# Arithmetic Operators

Operator	Description	Example
+	Adds two values together	x = 5 + 3
—	Subtracts one value from another	x = 7 − 5
*	Multiplies two values together	x = 3 * 10
/	Divides one value by another	x = 25 / 5
%	Divides one number into another and returns the modulus (remainder)	x = 10 % 3
x++	Post-increment (returns x, then increments x by one)	x = y++
++ x	Pre-increment (increments x by one, then returns x)	x = ++y
x −	Post-decrement (returns x, then decrements x by one)	x = y-
− x	Pre-decrement (decrements x by one, then returns x)	x = -y

statement executed, the value assigned to bonusPoints would be incremented by 1 and then this new value would be assigned to totalScore.

```
PlayerLives = ++BonusLives;
```

If you replace the x++ operator with the ++x operator, as demonstrated here, you will get a different result.

```
PlayerLives = BonusLives++;
```

This time, the value of BonusLives is assigned to PlayerLives before it is incremented and not after. As you would expect, the -x and x- operators work just like the ++x and x++ operators except that they decrement a value instead of increment it.

Assigning Variable Values

As you have already seen, you can assign a value to a variable using the = (equals) operator. Using the = operator, you can update a variable's value whenever required, as demonstrated here:

```
playerScore = 0;
```

.
.
.

```
playerScore = 100;
```

C# supports a number of other operators in addition to the = operator, as shown in Table 4.4.

Table 4.4 C# Assignment Operators

Operator	Description	Examples
=	Assigns a value	x = y + 1
+=	Shorthand for x = x + y	x += y
-=	Shorthand for x = x - y	x -= y
*=	Shorthand for x = x * y	x *= y
/=	Shorthand for x = x / y	x /= y
%=	Shorthand for x = x % y	x %= y

To better understand the use of the additional assignment operators listed in Table 4.4, look at the following example.

```
var x = 5;

x += 8;   // x now equals 8
x -= 2;   // x now equals 6
x *= 3;   // x now equals 18
x /= 2;   // x now equals 9
x %= 2;   // x now equals 1
```

Comparing Variable Values

In order to analyze data, you need to be able to compare it. When working with numeric data, this means comparing two values to determine if one is greater than, less than, or equal to the other value. Using the results of a comparison operation, C# can alter the logical execution of a program based on the data it is provided. Table 4.5 provides a list of comparison operators supported by C#.

In order to determine whether two values are equal, you can use the == operator. Note that this operator is not the same as the = (equals) operator. Don't mix up these two operators or else you'll get an error. To better understand how to work with C#'s comparison operators, consider the following example.

```
if (PlayerLives == 0)
{
    GameOver = true;
}
```

Table 4.5 C# Comparison Operators

Operator	Description	Example
==	Equal to	x == y
!==	Not equal to	x !== y
>	Greater than	x > y
>=	Greater than or equal to	x >= y
<	Less than	x < y
<=	Less than or equal to	x <= y

In this example, a comparison is made to determine if the value assigned to a variable named `PlayerLives` is equal to zero. If it is, the value or a variable named `GameOver` is set equal to `true`.

C# Keywords

C# keywords, also referred to as reserved words, have a special meaning and purpose in the C# programming language. As such, you cannot use them when assigning names to identifiers (e.g., variable, array, function names, etc.).

Trick

If you really want to, you can use any of the keywords listed above as an identifier's name, provided you precede the identifier name with the @ character (e.g., `@continue`, `@if`, `@else`).

Table 4.6 C# Keywords

abstract	as	base	bool
break	byte	case	catch
char	checked	class	const
continue	decimal	default	delegate
do	double	else	enum
event	explicit	extern	false
finally	fixed	float	for
foreach	goto	if	implicit
in	int	interface	internal
is	lock	long	namespace
new	null	object	operator
out	override	params	private
protected	public	readonly	ref
return	sbyte	sealed	short
sizeof	stackalloc	static	string
struct	switch	this	throw
true	try	typeof	uint
ulong	unchecked	unsafe	ushort
using	virtual	volatile	void
while			

Summary

In this chapter, you began learning how to program using C#. You learned a little about basic C# syntax and the different types of data supported by C#. You learned that constants store data when their value is known at design time and never changes. You learned how to store data that changes in variables and to create both local and global variables. You also learned how to store and process collections of data using arrays. This chapter also explained how to work with different types of C# operators, including assignment, arithmetic, and comparison operators. In Chapter 5, you will build upon your understanding of C# by learning how to apply conditional logic and setting up loops to perform repetitive tasks.

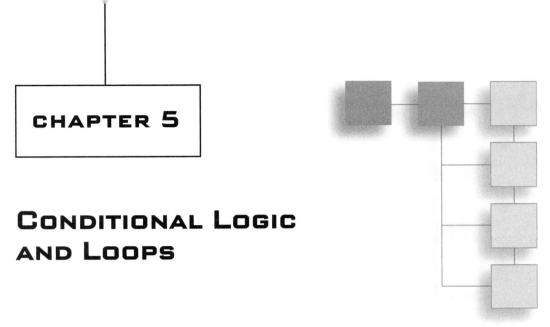

CHAPTER 5

CONDITIONAL LOGIC AND LOOPS

In the previous chapter, you learned the basics of C# syntax and the different types of data that C# can work with. You also learned how to store data using constants, variables, and arrays and to compare and analyze it using various C# operators. In this chapter, you will further expand your knowledge of C# programming by learning how to use conditional programming logic to analyze data and control program execution. You will then learn how to create and use loops to perform repetitive actions.

An overview of the major topics covered in this chapter includes learning how to:

- Use different variations of the if statement to analyze data

- Use the switch statements to compare data against a range of values

- Set up loops using the for, foreach, do, and while statements

Creating an XNA Template Application

This chapter will demonstrate the execution of a number of different types of programming statements. In order to be able to better understand the usage of these statements, it helps to have a working example that can display results on the screen when it executes. In this section, you are going to create an XNA application that can be used as the basis for testing and experimenting with all of the examples that are presented in this chapter.

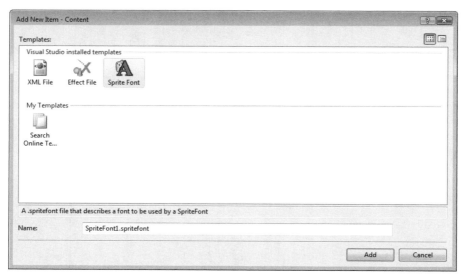

Figure 5.1
Adding a Sprite Font in order to be able to display text in an XNA application.

To set things up, you are going to need to create and customize a new XNA project that is capable of displaying text as it is executed. Once created, you will be able to adapt this application to run any of the examples presented in this chapter. The following procedures outline the steps involved in creating this new XNA application.

1. Click on File > New Project and then select Windows Game (3.1). Name the project Template and then click on OK.

2. In order to be able to display text, you need to add a Sprite Font to the application. This is done by going into Solution Explorer, right-clicking on Content, and then clicking on Add > New Item. The Add new Item – Content window appears, as shown in Figure 5.1.

Hint

A *sprite* is a graphics representation of an object within a computer game. A sprite can be a graphic image or a graphic text.

3. Select the Sprite Font Icon and click on Add. XNA will add a Sprite Font named SpriteFont1.spritefont to the project.

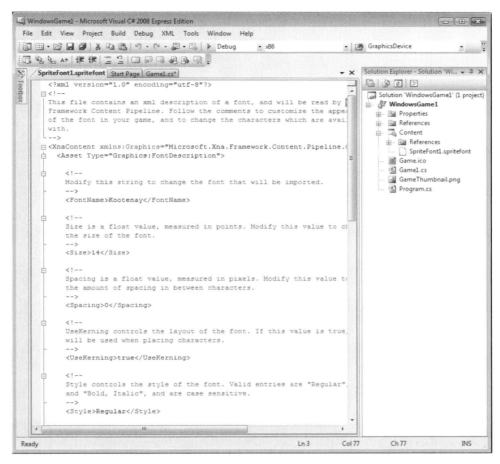

Figure 5.2
You can edit the Sprite Font in order to affect its type, size, appearance, and various other properties.

4. The contents of the new Sprite Font file are displayed in the code editor in the form of an XML file, as demonstrated in Figure 5.2. If you look closely at the file you will see entries that you can modify that affect the selection of the font and set its attributes. Leave the default font type of Kootenay in place and change its size from 14 to 20 by overtyping the values specified in between the <Size> and </Size> tags.

Hint

XML is a markup language used to facilitate the exchange of structured data between applications.

5. Close the SpriteFont1.spritefont file.

6. Next, you need to define a pair of global variables. To do so, add the
   following variable declaration statement to the beginning of the `Game1` class
   (just after the `SpriteBatch spriteBatch;` statement).

```
SpriteFont font;
String Msg;
```

The first statement shown here creates a `SpriteFont` variable named `font`
that will be used to store a reference to the Sprite Font that you just added to
the application. The second statement creates a `String` variable named `Msg`
which will be used by some examples to store and display string output.

7. Add the following statement to the `LoadContent()` method.

```
font = Content.Load<SpriteFont>("SpriteFont1");
```

This statement uses the `font` variable to load the font you previously loaded into
the project and to use the `font` variable to reference it.

Okay, you now have an XNA application that you can use as a template for
testing any of the examples presented in this chapter. The examples in this
chapter rely on the display of text to demonstrate the use of various programming constructs. To demonstrate its use, make a copy of the application
(remember, by default you will find your XNA applications in your Documents
folder in Documents\Visual Studio 2008\Projects) by copying and renaming its
folder. Using this copy, replace the contents of the `Draw()` method with the
statements shown here.

```
protected override void Draw(GameTime gameTime)
{
    GraphicsDevice.Clear(Color.White);
    Vector2 textVector = new Vector2(20, 20);

    spriteBatch.Begin();
    spriteBatch.DrawString(font, "Hello World!", textVector, Color.Blue);
    spriteBatch.End();

    base.Draw(gameTime);
}
```

This example merits additional explanation. It contains a number of new
statements that you have not seen before and these statements will be used

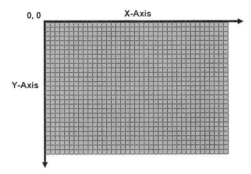

Figure 5.3
XNA coordinate system for two-dimensional graphics.

time and time again throughout this chapter. You have already seen the first statement in the method. It uses the GraphicsDevice class's Clear() method to clear the screen using the specified color. In order to draw text on the screen, you must use a vector that tells the Draw() method where to begin drawing the text. A *vector* is a mechanism for specifying the coordinates. In a 2D application, coordinates are mapped out using a coordinates system as demonstrated in Figure 5.3.

To create a vector, you must add an instance of the Vector2 (a 2D vector) object to your application. This is done above by defining a variable named textVector. Note that when you create a Vector2 object, you must supply the X and Y coordinates where the text should begin drawing.

NXA provides a class named SpriteBatch that can be used to draw sprites. XNA automatically adds an instance of the SpriteBatch class to every new project (in the LoadContent() method). Using the SpriteBatch class's Begin() method you can begin executing drawing commands. To use the DrawString() method, you must tell it what font to use, the text you want to display, and supply it with the property coordinates and the color to use when displaying it. The End() method marks the end of drawing operations.

Trap

Most of the examples shown in this chapter are based on the placement of various programming statements in the Draw() method. This has been done to facilitate learning and to simplify the presentation of examples. However, this is not an ideal scenario. It is strongly advised that you only place programming statements responsible for drawing in the Draw() method and that other programming statements be placed within the Update() method.

Analyzing Data and Making Decisions

Computer games involve the collection and processing of a lot of information. Data may, for example, be embedded within C# programs or it may be retrieved from external files. One thing is for certain, a lot of data comes directly from the player, providing it via the gamepad, keyword, etc. All of this data needs to be processed and analyzed. The mechanism for doing this is conditional programming logic. Conditional programming logic provides C# programs with the ability to make decisions based on the data they are presented with. To perform conditional logic you need to learn how to work with the `if` and `switch` statements along with the comparison operators that you learned about in Chapter 4.

Implementing Conditional Logic Using the if Statement

The primary programming statement used to implement conditional programming logic is the `if` statement. It allows you to compare two values and to control the execution of one or more statements based on that analysis. In its simplest form, the `if` statement is written as a single statement using the following syntax.

```
if (condition) statement;
```

Here, *condition* is an expression that when analyzed generates a `true` or `false` value, and *statement* is a C# statement that will be executed in the event that the tested condition evaluates as being true. Note that *condition* must be enclosed in parentheses. To better understand how to work with the `if` statement, look at the following example.

```
protected override void Update(GameTime gameTime)
{
    // Allows the game to exit
    if (GamePad.GetState(PlayerIndex.One).Buttons.Back ==
        ButtonState.Pressed)
        this.Exit();

    bool gameOver = true;
    if (gameOver == true) this.Exit();

    base.Update(gameTime);
}
```

In this example, a Boolean variable named gameOver is declared within the Update() method. A value of true is assigned to gameOver. Next, an if statement has been set up to analyze the value assigned to gameOver. Since gameOver is equal to true the statement this.Exit() is executed. To test the execution of this example, replace the statements that make up the Update() method in the model XNA application you created at the beginning of this chapter with those shown here, and then run the application. When you do, the application will start and then immediately terminate when the Exit() method executes.

Hint

In C#, the keyword this is a reference to the current object, providing a shortcut way of referring to it. In the previous example, this referred to the currently executing instance of the game class, which supports a method called Exit(). This method closes the game window and terminates the execution of the game in an orderly manner.

Using Multiline if Statements

If you need to execute more than one statement as a result of a conditional analysis, then you can use the { and } characters to group those statements into a code block, which can then be executed. For example, look at the following set of statements, which analyzes the value assigned to a variable named playerScore.

```
protected override void Draw(GameTime gameTime)
{
    GraphicsDevice.Clear(Color.White);
    Vector2 textVector = new Vector2(20, 20);

    spriteBatch.Begin();

    int playerScore = 100;
    if (playerScore > 50)
    {
        playerScore = 0;
        spriteBatch.DrawString(font, "Game Over!", textVector,
          Color.Blue);
    }
    spriteBatch.End();

    base.Draw(gameTime);
}
```

As you can see, the value of `playerScore` is arbitrarily set to 100. The value of `playerScore` is then analyzed to see if it is greater than 50, which of course it is. This being the case, all of the statements embedded in the `if` statement code block are executed. Had the value of `playerScore` been less than or equal to 50, the evaluation would have proved `false` and the code statements in the code block would not have been executed.

To test the execution of this example, create a copy of the XNA Template application that you created at the beginning of this chapter and then replace the statements that make up the `Draw()` method with those shown here, and then run the application.

Specifying Alternative Conditions

In the previous examples, the `if` statement was used to set up a conditional test that executed one or more embedded statements in the event a tested conditional evaluates as `true`. But what if you want to execute a different set of statements in the event the evaluated condition proves `false`? The solution is to add the optional `else` keyword to the `if` statement code block, as demonstrated in the following example.

```
protected override void Draw(GameTime gameTime)
{
    GraphicsDevice.Clear(Color.White);
    Vector2 textVector = new Vector2(20, 20);

    spriteBatch.Begin();

    int playerScore = 100;

    if (playerScore <= 500)
    {
        spriteBatch.DrawString(font, "Game Over. You lose.",
          textVector, Color.Blue);
    }
    else
    {
        spriteBatch.DrawString(font, "Game Over. You win.",
          textVector, Color.Blue);
    }
```

```
        spriteBatch.End();

        base.Draw(gameTime);
}
```

Here, `playerScore` has been set to `100` and then a conditional statement is set up to analyze the value of `playerScore` to see if it is less than or equal to 500. If it is, a message is displayed telling the player that he lost. If `playerScore` is greater than 500, a different message is displayed as specified in the `else` portion of the conditional text.

Again, to test the execution of this example, create a copy of the XNA Template application that you created at the beginning of this chapter and then replace the statements that make up the `Draw()` method with those shown here, and then run the application.

Evaluating Additional Conditions

If you need to you can expand upon the logic of your conditional text by including the `else if` keywords. The `else if` keywords allow you to evaluate and test different conditions, as demonstrated here:

```
protected override void Draw(GameTime gameTime)
{
    GraphicsDevice.Clear(Color.White);
    Vector2 textVector = new Vector2(20, 20);

    spriteBatch.Begin();

    int playerScore = 250;

    if (playerScore >= 100 && playerScore <= 199)
    {
        spriteBatch.DrawString(font,
          "Game Over. Your rank is beginner.", textVector, Color.Blue);
    }
    else if (playerScore >= 200)
    {
        spriteBatch.DrawString(font,
          "Game Over. Your rank is advanced.", textVector, Color.Blue);
    }
    else
```

```
    {
        spriteBatch.DrawString(font,
          "Game Over. You have not earned a rank.",
          textVector, Color.Blue);
    }

    spriteBatch.End();

    base.Draw(gameTime);
}
```

As you can see, this example first performs a check to see if playerScore is greater than or equal to 100 and less than or equal to 199. If this evaluation proves false, a second evaluation is performed to see if playerScore is greater and or equal to 200. If this evaluation proves false, then the statement located in the else code block is executed.

Nesting Multiple if Statements

As powerful as the different variations of the if statement can be, there are times when you will need to set up more complex conditional logic, involving the comparison of multiple values, where one decision is based on the outcome of another decision. To set up this kind of conditional logic, you need to embed or nest if statements within one another. The following example demonstrates how this works.

```
protected override void Draw(GameTime gameTime)
{
    GraphicsDevice.Clear(Color.White);
    Vector2 textVector = new Vector2(20, 20);

    spriteBatch.Begin();

    bool gameOver = false;
    int playerScore = 100;
    if (gameOver == true)
        {
        if (playerScore <= 10000) {
            spriteBatch.DrawString(font, "Game Over. You lose.",
                textVector, Color.Blue);
        }
```

```
        else {
            spriteBatch.DrawString(font, "Game Over. You win.",
              textVector, Color.Blue);
        }
    }
    else {
        spriteBatch.DrawString(font, "Please try again.",
          textVector, Color.Blue);
    }
    spriteBatch.End();

    base.Draw(gameTime);
}
```

In this example, the value of gameOver is analyzed to see if it is true. If it is, a nested if statement is executed to check if the value of totalScore is less than or equal to 10000. If totalScore is not less than or equal to 10000 then the statement located in the else portion of the embedded code block is executed. However, if the value assigned to gameOver proved false, the nested if statement is never executed and the else portion of the first if statement code block is executed.

Implementing Conditional Logic Using the switch Statement

Another way of implementing conditional logic is to set up a switch statement code block, which lets you compare the results of an expression against a series of possible matches. The syntax that you need to follow when working with the switch is outlined below.

```
switch (expression) {
  case label:
    statements;
    break;
    .
    .
    .
  case label:
    statements;
    break;
  default:
   statements;
    break;
}
```

The switch statement evaluates an expression and compares the results against a series of case statements to see if a match can be found. The value of *expression* is compared to the value of each case statement's *label*, which itself is just an expression. The statements belonging to the first case statement matches are executed. If a match is not found, the statements belonging to the optional default statement, if specified, get executed.

Note the use of the break statement to mark the end of the list of statements belonging to each case statement. The break statement is optional. If specified, the break statement instructs C# to exit the switch statement. If the break statement is not included, the program will execute the statements belonging to all case statements. As a result, more than one match may occur. The following example demonstrates how to work with the switch statement.

```
protected override void Draw(GameTime gameTime)
{
    GraphicsDevice.Clear(Color.White);
    Vector2 textVector = new Vector2(20, 20);

    spriteBatch.Begin();

    String character = "Wizard";
    switch (character)
    {
        case "Knight":
            spriteBatch.DrawString(font, "Welcome Sir knight!",
                textVector, Color.Blue);
            break;
        case "Wizard":
            spriteBatch.DrawString(font, "Welcome great wizard!",
                textVector, Color.Blue);
            break;
        case "Troll":
            spriteBatch.DrawString(font, "Welcome wise troll!",
                textVector, Color.Blue);
            break;
        default:
            spriteBatch.DrawString(font, "Error: unknown character.",
                textVector, Color.Blue);
            break;
    }
```

```
    spriteBatch.End();

    base.Draw(gameTime);
}
```

Here, a `switch` statement code block is used to execute one of a number of different statements depending on the value assigned to the `character` variable.

Again, to test the execution of this example, create a copy of the XNA Template application that you created at the beginning of this chapter and then replace the statements that make up the `Draw()` method with those shown here, and then run the application.

Processing Data Efficiently with Loops

Computer games must be able to process large amounts of data, quickly and efficiently. To do this, you must use loops. A *loop* is a collection of statements that get repeatedly executed. Loops let you process unlimited amounts of data using an absolute minimum number of statements. C# supports a number of different types of loops, including the `for`, `while`, `do`, and `foreach` loops.

Using the for Loop

The `for` loop executes as long as a specified condition evaluates as `true`. The execution of the `for` loop is controlled via variables. The loop's syntax is outlined here:

```
for (expression; condition; increment)
{
  statements;
}
```

The `for` loop consists of three parts, including a starting expression, a tested condition, and an increment statement. The statements embedded in between the loop's opening and closing brackets are executed every time the loop repeats or iterates. To better understand how the `for` loop works, look at the following example.

```
protected override void Draw(GameTime gameTime)
{
    GraphicsDevice.Clear(Color.White);
```

```
int x = 20;
int y = 20;

spriteBatch.Begin();

for (int i = 1; i <= 10; i++)
{
    Vector2 textVector = new Vector2(x, y);
    Msg = i.ToString();
    spriteBatch.DrawString(font, Msg, textVector, Color.Blue);
    y = y + 30;
}

spriteBatch.End();

base.Draw(gameTime);
}
```

Here, a for loop is set up to iterate 10 times. As you can see, the loop defines a variable named i, setting its starting value to 1. The loop iterates a total of 10 times, terminating once the value of i exceeds 10. Each time the loop repeats, the value of i is incremented by 1. Figure 5.4 shows the output produced when this example runs.

Figure 5.4
The XNA application counts from 1 to 10.

Using the while Loop

Using C#'s while loop, you can set up a loop that will execute as long as a specified condition is true. The syntax for the while loop is outlined here:

```
while (condition)
{
  statements;
}
```

The following example demonstrates the use of the while loop.

```
protected override void Draw(GameTime gameTime)
{
    GraphicsDevice.Clear(Color.White);

    int x = 20;
    int y = 20;
    int counter = 1;

    spriteBatch.Begin();

    while (counter <= 10)
    {
        Vector2 textVector = new Vector2(x, y);
        Msg = counter.ToString();
        spriteBatch.DrawString(font, Msg, textVector, Color.Blue);
        y = y + 30;
        counter++;      }
    spriteBatch.End();

    base.Draw(gameTime);
}
```

Here, a while loop has been set up to iterate for as long as the value of a variable named counter is less than or equal to 10. Each time the loop iterates, the value of counter is drawn to the screen and then incremented by 1.

The results produced when this example is processed are identical to the results from the for loop example. As you can see, you can use different types of loops to perform the same tasks. Despite this, each loop is better suited to specific circumstances. For example, the foreach loop, discussed a little later, is best used in processing the contents of lists and arrays, whereas the while loop is better used to set up a loop that has no specific predefined end but which executes for as long as a specific value or expression remains true.

Using the do Loop

C# also supports the use of the do loop, which executes repeatedly for as long as a tested condition remains true. The do loop has the following syntax.

```
do
{
    statements;
} while (condition)
```

The do loop always executes at least once since the loop's *condition* is not evaluated until the end of the loop. To better understand how this loop works, take a look at the following example.

```
protected override void Draw(GameTime gameTime)
{
    GraphicsDevice.Clear(Color.White);

    int x = 20;
    int y = 20;
    int counter = 10;

    spriteBatch.Begin();

    do
    {
        Vector2 textVector = new Vector2(x, y);
        Msg = counter.ToString();
        spriteBatch.DrawString(font, Msg, textVector, Color.Blue);
        y = y + 30;
        counter-;
    } while (counter >= 1);

    spriteBatch.End();

    base.Draw(gameTime);
}
```

Here, a do loop has been set up to repeat for as long as the value of counter is greater than or equal to 1. As Figure 5.5 shows, this loop executes 10 times, counting backwards from 10 to 1.

Figure 5.5
Using a do loop to count backwards.

Using the foreach Loop

The foreach loop is designed to process lists of data returned by commands or stored in arrays. Rather than iterating a specified number of times like the for loop or until a specified condition evaluates as true like the while and do loops, the foreach loop repeats once for each item in a list, using the following syntax:

```
foreach (type in list)
{
    statements;
}
```

The following example demonstrates how to work with the foreach statement.

```
protected override void Draw(GameTime gameTime)
{
    GraphicsDevice.Clear(Color.White);

    int x = 20;
    int y = 20;

    spriteBatch.Begin();
```

```
string[] SuperPowers = new string[3];
SuperPowers[0] = "Flight";
SuperPowers[1] = "Super Strength";
SuperPowers[2] = "Invisibility";

foreach (string power in SuperPowers)
{
    Vector2 textVector = new Vector2(x, y);
    spriteBatch.DrawString(font, power, textVector, Color.Blue);
    y = y + 30;
}

spriteBatch.End();

base.Draw(gameTime);
}
```

Here, a loop has been set up to process the contents stored in an array named SuperPowers. Note that the loop includes the definition of a string variable named power. Since the array contains three items, the loop will iterate three times. Each time the loop iterates, it processes a different item stored in the array, assigning its value to the power variable. Figure 5.6 shows the output that is displayed when this example executes.

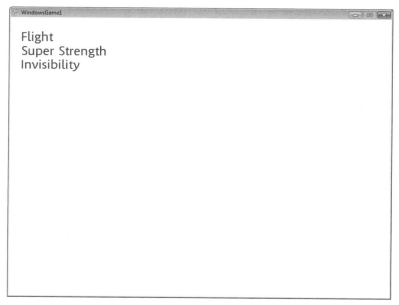

Figure 5.6
Using a `foreach` loop to process the contents of an array.

Altering Normal Loop Execution

By default, a loop executes every statement embedded within it as many times as specified. However, there may be times where you want to alter this execution flow. For example, you might want to terminate a loop's execution in the event invalid data is received or if the player signals your game to terminate. The following example demonstrates how to use the break statement to prematurely halt a loop's execution.

```
protected override void Draw(GameTime gameTime)
{
    GraphicsDevice.Clear(Color.White);

    int x = 20;
    int y = 20;

    spriteBatch.Begin();

    for (int i = 1; i <= 10; i++)
    {
        Vector2 textVector = new Vector2(x, y);
        Msg = i.ToString();
        spriteBatch.DrawString(font, Msg, textVector, Color.Blue);
        y = y + 30;
        if (i == 5) break;
    }

    spriteBatch.End();

    base.Draw(gameTime);
}
```

As demonstrated in Figure 5.7, the loop outlined in this example is halted when the value of i is set equal to 5.

Similarly, you can use the continue statement to halt the current iteration of a loop without terminating the loop's execution. To see how to work with the continue keyword, look at the following example.

```
protected override void Draw(GameTime gameTime)
{
    GraphicsDevice.Clear(Color.White);
```

```
int x = 20;

int y = 20;

spriteBatch.Begin();

for (int i = 1; i <= 10; i++)
{
    Vector2 textVector = new Vector2(x, y);
    if (i == 3 || i == 5 || i == 7) continue;
    Msg = i.ToString();
    spriteBatch.DrawString(font, Msg, textVector, Color.Blue);
    y = y + 30;
}

spriteBatch.End();

base.Draw(gameTime);
}
```

Figure 5.7
Using the break keyword to prematurly halt a loop's execution.

Hint

Note the use of the || characters in the previous example. These characters specify a logical operator that you can use to combine comparison operations, creating a compound expression that evaluates as true in the event that either one of the tested conditions proves true.

Table 5.1 C# Logical Operators

Operator	Description
&&	Returns a Boolean value of true if both values evaluate as true
||	Returns a Boolean value of true if either value evaluates as true
!	Reverses the value assigned to a Boolean value

When executed, this example displays the following output on the screen. As you can see in Figure 5.8, the 3rd, 5th, and 7th iteration of the for loop have been skipped.

Figure 5.8
Using the continue keyboard to skip a loop's iteration.

Summary

This chapter showed you how to use different variations of the if statement as a means of analyzing data and controlling the logical flow of programming logic in your NXA applications. You learned how to use the switch statement to compare a value to a range of possible matching values. You also learned how to set up a wide variety of different types of loops using the for, foreach, do, and while statements, giving you the ability to efficiently process large amounts of data and perform repetitive tasks. In Chapter 6 you will round out your C# programming knowledge by learning how to create and work with classes, objects, and their methods and properties.

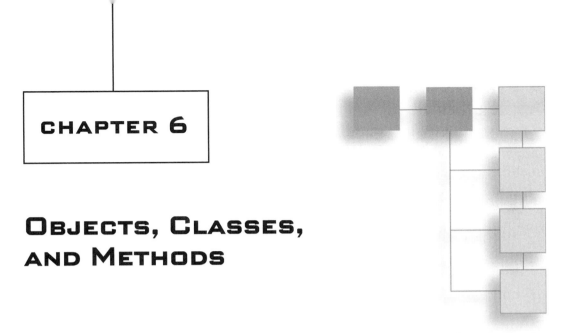

CHAPTER 6

OBJECTS, CLASSES, AND METHODS

This final chapter in Part II will round out your C# programming foundation by introducing you to concepts and terms associated with object-oriented programming. XNA games and applications, written using C#, are object-oriented so it is essential that you understand concepts like abstraction, encapsulation, inheritance, and polymorphism. You will also learn about classes and their use in the creation of objects. The XNA development environment provides access to numerous classes organized within namespaces. You'll learn about many of these namespaces and classes. On top of all this, you will learn how to define your own custom classes and to use those classes within your XNA games to create and control objects.

Specifically, you will learn:

- About namespaces and the program class

- About object-oriented programming concepts and terms

- How to define custom classes and to instantiate objects based on those classes

- How to provide controlled access to the data stored within objects

- How to define structures as an alternative to defining classes

A Deeper Look at the Inner Workings of XNA Applications

Your XNA games and applications are created by developing C# programs that interact with the user, responding to user input while controlling the movements and interaction of on-screen graphics as well as the playback of sound effects and background music. C# programs are made up of collections of statements. Related statements are grouped together into methods in order to perform specific tasks. A *method* is a named collection of statements that when called performs a specific task. Methods allow large programs to be organized into manageable sections.

Within your C# programs, methods are grouped within classes. When XNA creates a new game project, it automatically creates an instance of the Game1 class. A *class* is a construct that is used as a template or blueprint for adding objects to XNA applications. Classes define the data and methods that make up objects. Whenever an instance of a class is instantiated, the methods defined within that class are automatically loaded in memory.

Trick

If you want, you can rename the Game1 program to something more meaningful to you, thus making your program code more self-documenting. To do so, locate the Game1.cs entry in Solution Explorer and right-click on it, and then select the Rename option from the content menu that is displayed, as demonstrated in Figure 6.1.

Immediately after you rename Game1.cs, the popup dialog window shown in Figure 6.2 appears, prompting you for permission to rename all references to the file within your program code.

The Game1 class that XNA creates for you is generated within the Program.cs file, as shown here.

```
using System;

namespace WindowsGame1
{
    static class Program
    {
        static void Main(string[] args)
        {
            using (Game1 game = new Game1())
            {
                game.Run();
            }
```

Figure 6.1
Renaming the Game1 program to something more meaningful.

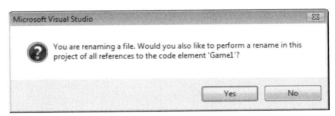

Figure 6.2
Click on Yes when prompted in order to keep things logically aligned within your application.

```
        }
    }
}
```

The Program.cs file is one of two C# programs created by XNA each time to create a new XNA project. This program's primary purpose is to create an instance of your XNA game and then run it. A detailed examination of the contents of this program is provided in the sections that follow.

The System Name Space

The first statement in the Program.cs file, shown next, is a compiler directive. A *compiler directive* is an instruction that tells the compiler to do something; in this case, the directive tells the compiler to use the System namespace.

```
using System;
```

A *namespace*, covered in the next section, is a library of class descriptions. In XNA applications, namespaces provide games with access to classes belonging to the .NET Framework. The System namespace contains a collection of base classes required by Windows applications, supporting such things as the definition of commonly used values and data types, program execution, and execution handling.

Namespaces

When you reference a class name within a program in an XNA application, the compiler looks for it in all of the namespaces that are defined within the application until it finds it. Of course, if the class is not found, an error occurs. One advantage of namespaces is that they prevent naming conflicts by allowing similarly named resources in different namespaces to happily coexist.

XNA automatically creates a new namespace for each application you create. This namespace is defined by a code block in the next set of statements in the Program.cs file, as shown here:

```
namespace WindowsGame1
{

}
```

Note that by default, XNA assigns the same name to this namespace that you assign to your application. If, however, you do not assign a name to your application, XNA will assign a name of WindowsGameX to it (X represents a numeric value that is automatically incremented each time you create a new unnamed application). All of the classes that you define within your XNA applications will be placed within this namespace (e.g., inside the Game1.cs file).

Hint

By default, the Game1.cs program in every new XNA application contains references to the collection of namespaces shown next. These namespace references are set up with compiler directives established with the using statement.

```
using System;
using System.Collections.Generic;
using System.Linq;
using Microsoft.Xna.Framework;
using Microsoft.Xna.Framework.Audio;
using Microsoft.Xna.Framework.Content;
```

```
using Microsoft.Xna.Framework.GamerServices;
using Microsoft.Xna.Framework.Graphics;
using Microsoft.Xna.Framework.Input;
using Microsoft.Xna.Framework.Media;
using Microsoft.Xna.Framework.Net;
using Microsoft.Xna.Framework.Storage;
```

The namespaces outlined here provide your XNA applications with access to essential resources needed to create computer games. For example, the Graphics namespace provides your games with access to classes that manipulate graphics. One such class that you will learn how to work with is the Texture2D class, which you'll use when displaying graphics in your games. Similarly, the Audio class provides access to resources needed to intergrate sound effects and music in your games.

In addition to the namespaces listed above, every new XNA application also contains a name-space that matches the name you assigned to your game. It is within this class that the Initialize(), LoadContent(), UnloadContent(), Update(), and Draw() methods are defined. You create new XNA games by adding your own programming logic to the methods in this class.

The Program Class

The next line in Program.cs defines a class named Program, as shown below. Note the use of the static keyword. When used, this keyword permits a single instance of the class to run. Static classes are always started first, after which the code you added to the Game1.cs program is run.

```
static class Program
{

}
```

The rest of the statements that make up the Program.cs program are all located within the Program class.

Methods

The Program class's primary purpose is to create an instance of your XNA game and then to run it. It accomplishes this by calling upon the program's Main method, which is accomplished through the execution of the Main() method shown here.

```
static void Main(string[] args)
{

}
```

The Main() method is of central importance to your XNA applications. Its job is to start game execution.

Hint

Note that the Main() method is set up to accept and process any number of string arguments passed to it. This is denoted through the specification of a parameter named args, which is a list of one or more strings. If you set up your XNA games to start from the Windows command prompt, you can execute them by typing in their names followed by a list of strings, which the game can then process as input. However, most games are not started this way, including those run on the Xbox 360 and Zune. As such, no arguments are passed to the game and this argument is never used.

Garbage Collection

Within the Program class's Main() method is an embedded code block created using the using statement. When used in this context, the using statement instructs the program to dispose of an object as soon as it finishes execution. This allows any data belonging to the object to be deleted from memory, freeing up resources for other tasks.

```
using (Game1 game = new Game1())
{

}
```

The object being referenced here is named game, which as you can see, is created using the new keyboard. This object is based on the Game1 class, which is defined within the Game1.cs file (unless, of course, you have changed its name).

Hint

As your XNA games execute, a progress known as garbage collection automatically keeps track of and removes unused resources. This helps make your XNA games and other applications run smoothly, by ensuring that resources are not needlessly allocated. To further streamline your XNA applications, you can use the using keyword as previously demonstrated, ensuring that unused resources are immediately made available once they are no longer needed.

Game Execution

The Main() method consists of a single statement to start the execution of your XNA game. This statement, shown next, executes the Game1 class's Run() method. The Run() method, as its name implies, initiates the execution of the game loop.

```
game.Run();
```

The Run() method begins by executing the Initialize() method followed by the LoadContent() method. It then repeatedly executes the Update() and Draw() methods.

Object-Oriented Programming

At this point, you should have a good overall understanding of how namespaces, classes, and objects work within XNA games and applications. With this understanding now in hand, you are ready to begin tackling more complex programming challenges including learning how to define your own classes and methods.

So far, this book has talked a lot about classes, objects, and methods. The inclusion and manipulation of these resources is done through a programming technique known as object-oriented programming. Whether you realize it or not, you have already been learning the fundamentals of object-oriented programming as you've made your way through to this point in the book.

In OOP (*object-oriented programming*) data and program code are managed together as a single unit in the form of objects. An object is a self-contained entity. Objects store data. Objects also contain methods that serve as an interface for interacting with it. Objects can validate data passed to them and can reject the data if it does not satisfy predefined criteria. Well-defined objects result in more reliable applications.

Important OOP Terms You Need to Know

In OOP, an object is created from a class. Classes serve as templates that outline the data, properties, and methods that make up the objects. OOP helps simplify the coding process. It promotes code reuse by letting you define a class once and then call on it repeatedly to create any number of new objects.

XNA provides access to a huge collection of classes. For example, to enable the playback of an audio sound effect within an XNA application, you'll need to create or instantiate an object based on the SoundEffect class. This class is made available to your XNA applications through the Microsoft.Xna.Framework.Audio namespace. Remember that a *namespace* is a collection of related classes. XNA and the .NET Framework provide access to many namespaces filled with classes.

You have been working with many different types of classes throughout this book. For example, one of the first statements in the Game1.cs file is shown next.

XNA automatically generates this class definition on your behalf. Within this class code block you will find the `Initialize()`, `LoadContent()`, `UnloadContent()`, `Update()`, and `Draw()` methods.

```
Public Class Game1
{


}
```

In addition to all of the various classes that XNA makes available to you, Visual C# also permits you to create your own custom classes. To learn how to do so, you must first learn a number of new programming concepts, including:

- Abstraction

- Encapsulation

- Inheritance

- Polymorphism

Abstraction

Abstraction is the process of defining a logical representation of a class within program code. This includes defining all the data members, properties, and methods required for the proper operation of the class and the objects derived from it. For example, if you were going to define a class representing a person, you might include `height`, `weight`, and `age` properties as well as methods like `talk()`, `walk()`, and `sit()`.

Encapsulation

Encapsulation is the process used to outline the base functionality of a class. It provides the ability to interact with objects created based on that class through the properties and methods defined within it. Encapsulation helps simplify things by eliminating the need to understand the inner workings of objects. Consider for example the `spriteBatch` class, which you have seen used to control the drawing of text to the screen. You do not know what the program code for this class looks like or how it is written and you do not need to. You can't directly access any of the internal code outlined in the `spriteBatch` class. All you need to know is what properties and methods are available. How the `spriteBatch` class is designed is masked from view. As such, encapsulation simplifies program development.

Encapsulation also provides data protection. As such, you can add program code to your classes that processes and verifies any data passed to objects in order to ensure that the data meets certain criteria. If it does not, the data can be rejected.

Inheritance

Inheritance is the process in which one class is derived from another (parent) class. Inheritance allows you to create a class hierarchy. For example, inheritance allows you to define a base class. An example of this would be a class that describes a generic automobile. This would include all of the properties required to describe the characteristics (e.g., 2-door, 4-door, color, etc.) of the automobile as well as all of its basic functionality (move, break, turn, etc.). With inheritance, you could then use this base class as the foundation for creating a new child class, which would inherit all of the properties and methods of its parent class. Further, you can extend the features of the child class by adding additional properties and methods to it.

Polymorphism

Polymorphism is a term that describes the ability to define different forms of the same thing. In C#, polymorphism is accomplished using a programming technique known as overloading. With o*verloading*, you define the same method two or more times. Each instance of the method must be assigned a different argument list. For example, overloading allows you to create different versions of the same method, all with the same name but with different combinations of arguments. One instance of the method might be designed to process a single integer argument, whereas another instance of the method might be set up to process two arguments, one integer, and one string.

Defining Your Own Classes and Objects

Classes serve as templates for defining the attributes, properties, and methods of objects. Using abstraction you develop the overall design of a class. Using encapsulation you implement its structure. With inheritance, one class can be used as the basis for another class. Finally, with overloading you can extend methods within your classes in order to allow them to process different sets of arguments.

Objects are instantiated based on classes. A helpful analogy for understanding this concept is to compare the relationship between a class and an object to that of a mold and Jell-O. A mold outlines an overall size and shape. Once poured into a mold and solidified, the new instance of Jell-O (e.g., object) assumes the basic qualities of the mold (e.g., class).

Creating a New Class

As you have already seen, anytime you create a new XNA game, a new class is created for you named Game1 and you can modify the methods and properties that make up this class. In addition, you can add a new class to an application by inserting its declaration under the existing class definition in the code editor, as shown here:

```
namespace WindowsGame1
{
    public class Game1 : Microsoft.Xna.Framework.Game
    {
        GraphicsDeviceManager graphics;
        SpriteBatch spriteBatch;

        public Game1()
        {
            graphics = new GraphicsDeviceManager(this);
            Content.RootDirectory = "Content";
        }

        protected override void Initialize()
        {
            base.Initialize();
        }

        protected override void LoadContent()
        {
            spriteBatch = new SpriteBatch(GraphicsDevice);
        }

        protected override void UnloadContent()
        {
        }

        protected override void Update(GameTime gameTime)
        {
            if (GamePad.GetState(PlayerIndex.One).Buttons.Back ==
                ButtonState.Pressed)
                this.Exit();
```

```
        base.Update(gameTime);
    }

    protected override void Draw(GameTime gameTime)
    {
        GraphicsDevice.Clear(Color.CornflowerBlue);
        base.Draw(gameTime);
    }
}

public class NameMgr
{
}

}
```

In this example, a new class named NameMgr has been defined. At the moment, the class does not have any data members, properties, or methods defined to it. A *data member* is a variable that is defined within a class. Each object that you instantiate based on the class inherits the class's variable definitions and can store its own data in its data members. This data is separate and distinct from the data that may be stored in other objects created from that same class.

Ordinarily, data members are hidden from the outside world and used only within the class. However, data members can be made directly accessible from outside the class by preceding their declaration with the Public keyword.

Hint

All class names must be unique within the same namespace. However, by defining classes in different namespaces, you can assign a class a name used within another namespace without causing any errors. Therefore, it is a good programming practice to define all of your classes within unique namespaces, thus ensuring they do not conflict with the names of classes defined elsewhere. XNA helps you do this by automatically creating a new namespace for you in the Game1.cs program. In the previous example, the default name assigned to the namespace was WindowsGame1. As such, to prevent an error from occurring, the NameMgr class must be uniquely named within this namespace.

Understanding Data Members

In the previous example, a new class named NameMgr was defined. However, the class is empty in that it does not specify anything yet. Let's change this by modifying the class as shown here.

```
public class NameMgr
{
    private string UserName;
}
```

Here, a *data member* has been defined within the class. Class data members are private. By default, a private data member is accessible only to methods within the class where it is defined. Since class members are private by default, you can eliminate the `private` keyword as shown here, but the result is still the same.

```
string UserName;
```

A private data member cannot be accessed from outside the class. If you want, you can make data members publicly available by preceding them with the `public` keyword, as shown here.

```
public string Name;
```

You can also make a data member protected using the `protected` keyword, as shown here.

```
protected string Name;
```

A *protected* data member is accessible to methods within a class and to methods in child classes but not to objects based on other classes.

Setting Up Class Properties

Data members can be accessed from outside the class in which they are defined. A data member is not, however, a property of a class. Publicly accessible data members mean that you lose the ability to control access to the data stored in them. Instead of creating public data members, it is better to make them private. You can then control access to the data stored within a class's data members through properties.

Rather than allow unrestricted access to public data members, you can use properties to control access to data stored within data members. To set up a property in a class, you must declare a data member private and then define a public property that can be used to control access to the value stored in the data member. C# supports the following types of property procedures.

- **get.** Retrieves the value assigned to a property.

- **set.** Assigns a value to a property.

The following example demonstrates how to add a property to a class.

```
public class NameMgr
{
    private string UserName;

    public string Name
    {
        get
        {
            return UserName;
        }
        set
        {
            UserName = value;
        }
    }
}
```

As you can see, access to the value stored in the UserName data member is made private. As a result, only methods defined within its class can access it. Two procedures are then set up to control access to the value stored in the data member. The first procedure allows the retrieval of the value stored in the data member and the second procedure allows that value to be modified.

Instantiating Objects

In order to use the NameMgr class, you must instantiate an object based on it. This is done using the new keyword, as demonstrated here:

```
NameMgr x = new NameMgr();
```

Once instantiated, you can store and retrieve a value using the UserName data member through the class's Name property. For example, the following statement demonstrates how to store a string value via the Name property.

```
x.Name = "Bob";
```

As you can see, the reference to the Name property is made by specifying the name of the object, followed by a period and the property name. When you assign a value to the Name property, the set property procedure executes. The set property procedure is passed an argument made up of the data that was assigned to the Name property. Within the set property procedure, the value of the argument is assigned to the data member (e.g., UserName). Similarly, if you later retrieve the `Name` property, the value of the data stored in the `UserName` data member is returned.

A primary advantage of using properties as means of indirectly accessing data members is that you can include programming logic that performs data validation before allowing a data member's value to be modified.

```
public class NameMgr
{
    private string UserName;

    public string Name
    {
        get
        {
            return UserName;
        }
        set
        {
            if (value.Length > 0)
            {
                UserName = value;
            }
        }
    }
}
```

This new example prevents an empty string from being assigned as the data member's value.

Adding Methods to Classes

In addition to data members and properties, you can also add methods to your custom classes. To add a method, all you have to do is add a method definition, as demonstrated here:

```
public class NameMgr
{
    private string UserName;

    public string Name
    {
        get
```

```
        {
            return UserName;
        }
        set
        {
            if (value.Length > 0)
            {
                UserName = value;
            }
        }
    }
    public string GenerateAddress()
    {
        return (UserName + "@yahoo.com");
    }
}
```

In this example, a method named GenerateAddress() has been modified. This method appends the string "@yahoo.com" to the value stored in the UserName data member and returns it when called. Within your program code, you execute this method just as you do with any other method by specifying the name of its object followed by a period and the method's name.

Overloading Methods

As already discussed, Visual C# supports polymorphism through a process referred to as overloading, whereby a method is defined two or more times with different sets of arguments. When you overload a method, as demonstrated below, Visual C# makes sure that the correct method is executed based on the argument list that is specified.

```
public class NameMgr
{
    private string UserName;

    public string Name
    {
        get
        {
            return UserName;
        }
        set
```

```
        {
            if (value.Length > 0)
            {
                UserName = value;
            }
        }
    }
    public string GenerateAddress()
    {
        return (UserName + "@yahoo.com");
    }
    public string GenerateAddress(string input)
    {
        return (input + "@yahoo.com");
    }
}
```

Here two different versions of the GenerateAddress() method have been defined. The first instance appends the string "@yahoo.com" to the value stored in the UserName data member and returns the result. This version of the Generate-Address() method is executed whenever the GenerateAddress() method is called without any arguments. The second version of the GenerateAddress() method is executed when the method is passed a single string argument. When executed it appends the string "@yahoo.com" to the argument string and returns the result.

Hint

In order for overloading to work, you must ensure that each method you define has a unique set of arguments. The argument list can be varied by number of arguments or by changing the types of arguments passed, or both.

Inheriting from Another Class

The derived class inherits its features from the base class. In addition to inheriting from classes provided to you by Visual C# and the .NET Framework, you can derive new classes from classes that you create. The following example demonstrates how to create a new class named NameMgrTwo using the NameMgr class as the base class.

```
public class NameMgr
{
    private string UserName;
    public string Name
```

```
    {
        get
        {
            return UserName;
        }
        set
        {
            if (value.Length > 0)
            {
                UserName = value;
            }
        }
    }
    public string GenerateAddress()
    {
        return (UserName + "@yahoo.com");
    }
}

public class NameMgrTwo : NameMgr
{
    public string GenerateAddress(string input)
    {
        return (input + "@yahoo.com");
    }
}
```

The `NameMgrTwo` class inherits all of the data member's properties and methods belonging to the `NameMgr` class and then extends its functionality by adding an additional method (overloading the `GenerateAddress()` method).

Structures

A class is a complex data structure that encapsulates data members, properties, and methods into a simple logical entity. C# also supports an alternate means of encapsulating data known as a structure. Classes are usually used to define complex entities whose data changes during program execution, while structures are usually used to define and manage small collections of related data. For example, in a game like *Pong*, in which a ball is bounced around the screen, a number of variables are involved in the movement of the ball. To be visible, the ball needs to be represented by a texture and it must be managed using a `rectangle`. The ball's location is specified by setting variables that represent its X and

Y coordinates. Its speed and direction must be set for both its X and Y coordinates. To set all this up, you might define the following variables as follows:

```
Texture2D BallTexture;
Rectangle BallRectangle;
Float BallX;
Float BallY;
Float BallSpeedX;
Float BallSpeedY;
```

Once defined, the program would need to constantly modify the values assigned to these variables in order to control the movement of the ball around the screen. Now, suppose you want to make the game more challenging by putting a second ball into play. You could do this by making a copy of the previous six variables and changing their names as demonstrated here:

```
Texture2D Ball2Texture;
Rectangle Ball2Rectangle;
Float Ball2X;
Float Ball2Y;
Float Ball2SpeedX;
Float Ball2SpeedY;
```

Now suppose you decided to add a third or fourth ball. As you can see, each additional ball results in a whole new set of variable declaration statements. A better way of handling this situation is to take advantage of C# structures. A *structure* is a group of data items that can be referenced by value. Structures make it easier to work in the data that needs to be managed in a coordinated manner, as demonstrated here:

Hint

Variables and objects are passed by reference. This means that if you pass a variable or object to a method and the method makes a change to the variable or object, the variable or object is changed. Structures are passed by value. What this means is that if you pass a structure to a method, a copy of the structure is passed and any changes made to that copy do not impact the structure as it exists outside the method. You can, however, use the ref keyword to override this behavior and pass a structure by reference.

```
Struct BallStructure
{
    public Texture2d BallTexture;
    public Rectangle BallRectangle;
    public float BallX;
```

```
    public float BallY;
    public Float SpeedY;
    public Float SpeedX;
}
```

Here, a structure has been defined using the Struct keyword. Each of the items defined within the structure is referenced as a field. Once defined, you can use the structure to add additional balls to your game, as shown here:

```
BallStructure BallRed;
BallStructure BallBlue;
BallStructure BallGreen;
```

Here three separate balls are created. Once a structure variable is declared, you can access all of the fields within the structure and begin assigning data to them and retrieving data from them. For example, to begin storing data within the BallRed structure variable, all you have to do is use dot notation, as demonstrated here:

```
BallRed.BallTexture = Content.Load<Texture2D>("Ball");
BallRed.BallRectangle.Width = 20.0f;
BallRed.BallRectangle.Height = 5.0f;
BallRed.BallX = displayWidth / 2;
BallRed.BallY = displayHeight / 2;
BallRed.SpeedY = 10.0f;
BallRed.SpeedX = 10.0f;
```

Likewise, you can assign data to the BallBlue and BallGreen structures. Structures are commonly used features in many XNA games and you will see more examples of how to work with them later in this book. For now, all you need to understand is that structures let you group related collections of variables and methods together and pass them as a unit for processing, and that they are better suited than classes when defining simple data structures.

Summary

In this chapter, you learned about object-oriented programming concepts like abstractions, encapsulation, inheritance, and polymorphism. You learned about namespaces and classes and examined construction of the Game1 class. You also learned how to define and work with your own custom classes. Lastly, you learned how to use structures as an alternative to classes when designing and working with small groups of related data.

PART III

GAME DEVELOPMENT BASICS

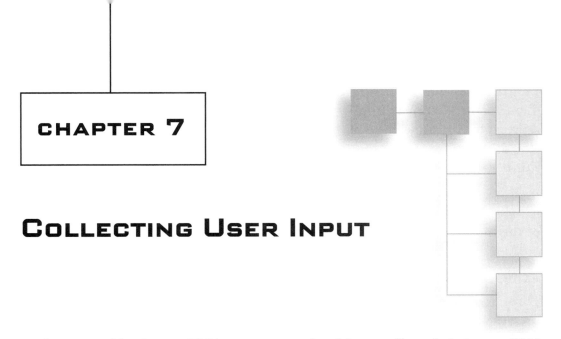

CHAPTER 7

COLLECTING USER INPUT

To interact with players, XNA games must be able to collect their input. XNA provides you with everything you need to develop PC and Xbox games that can interact with players using either a keyboard or gamepad controllers. XNA lets you create games on the Zune, using the Zune button and joypad controller. This chapter will identify the XNA classes that support interaction with different game controllers and show you how to work with them.

An overview of the major topics covered in this chapter includes learning how to:

- Detect gamepads and react when the player presses buttons

- Collect user input using the gamepad thumbpads and the Dpad

- Collect user keyboard input

- Collect input when your games are played on the Zune

Using Game Input

All computer games require a means of interacting with players, whether it is through gamepads, a keyboard, a mouse, or some combination of devices. XNA provides programmers with several classes designed to support interaction with various input devices. These classes include the GamePad, Keyboard, and Mouse classes, which as you can guess, provide access to methods and properties that let you interact with gamepads, keyboard, and the mouse. These classes are all made available through the Microsoft.Xna.Framework.Input namespace.

Input devices are made up of two different types of controls, digital and analog. A digital control is one that reports either of two states (on or off). These states are represented by Boolean values of true or false. For example, the gamepad's X, Y, B, A, Back, and Start buttons are all digital controls. Likewise, the buttons on a Zune player, mouse, and all of the keys on a keyboard are also digital controls.

Analog controls differ from digital controls in that they report a range of values. Examples of analog controls include the gamepad thumbpads and the movement of the mouse.

Collecting Player Input

Throughout game play, players interact with the game through input devices like the gamepad, mouse, and keyboard. In order to collect player input, the game must poll its controls. *Polling* is the process of repeatedly querying a game control's state and processing its data. This is accomplished by placing statements within the application's update() method that collect and process game state.

Hint

XNA provides access to all input devices, regardless of which platform your games run on. As a result, you can attempt to programmatically access the mouse even when your games run on the Zune or Xbox 360, which do not support either of these devices. However, XNA will not be able to return any data for these devices. Keep this in mind as you develop your games.

Platform-Supported Controllers

As mentioned, XNA supports interaction with various types of devices, varied by platform. Table 7.1 lists all of the major types of controls supported by XNA, showing you which ones are available on which platform.

You can use a wired USB Xbox 360 gamepad on any computer running Windows XP, Windows Vista, or Windows 7. Simply plug it into an available USB port and

Table 7.1 Supported Input Devices

Device	Windows	Xbox 360	Zune
Xbox 360 gamepad	Y	Y	Limited
Mouse	Y	N	N
Keyboard	Y	Y	N

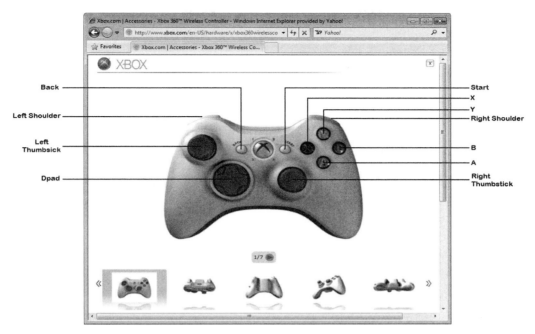

Figure 7.1
The gamepad controller can collect player input via an assortment of buttons, two thumbsticks, and a Dpad.

Windows will automatically detect it, load the appropriate software drivers, and install the device. Once installed, your PC-based XNA games can interact in the exact same way that your XNA games do on the Xbox 360. Similarly, you can plug a USB keyboard into an Xbox 360 and it will work with it as well. The Xbox 360 does not, however, support the use of a mouse. Nor does the Zune. XNA maps the Xbox 360 gamepad to the Zune player's Zune Pad control, resulting in support for a subset of the gamepad's controls.

Although not all devices are supported by all platforms, the APIs (application programming interfaces) for those devices remain available. Therefore, even though the Zune does not support either a mouse or a keyboard, program code that references these devices does not generate an error, nor can it retrieve any data.

Collecting Gamepad Input

Gamepads are excellent game controllers. Both the Xbox 360 and Windows computers can support as many as four gamepad controllers at a time. The gamepad consists of a collection of analog and digital controls, in the forms of buttons, thumbsticks, and a Dpad. This collection of controls makes the gamepad an excellent controller for playing most types of games.

Hint

Dpad stands for directional pad (sometimes referred to as a joypad) and is a four-point, plus-shaped control that allows for up/down/left/right input.

Figure 7.1 shows the collections of controls provided by a gamepad controller.

Hint

To use a gamepad on your Windows XP or Vista computer all you have to do is attach a USB-wired gamepad to one of your computer's USB connections. In response, Windows will automatically load the drivers needed to let your computer interact with the gamepad.

Once a connection is established to a gamepad, XNA can interact with it in both directions, retrieving data from it and sending instructions to it. Data retrieved from a gamepad includes coordinate data supplied by thumbsticks, as well as state information provided by button presses. Conversely, you can enable the vibration on gamepad controllers in order to provide game feedback to players.

Gamepad data is provided in XNA applications via the GamePadState class. The GamePadState class is used in conjunction with the GamePad class to set up connections to gamepad controllers. The GamePad class has a method called GetState() which is used to retrieve the state information from a gamepad controller. When called, you must pass the GetState() method a parameter identifying the gamepad being referenced, as demonstrated here:

Hint

XNA can work with as many as four gamepads at a time. You physically can identify a gamepad's assigned number by examining the position of the green light that is lit up around the gamepad's power button.

```
GamePadState gamePadOne = GamePad.GetState(PlayerIndex.One);
```

Gamepad Buttons

Once you have retrieved state data for a gamepad, you can use it as input for your XNA game, as demonstrated in the following example.

```
if (pad1.Buttons.Start == ButtonState.Pressed)
{
    //Do something here
}
```

Here, a check is made to determine if the player is pressing the gamepad's Start button.

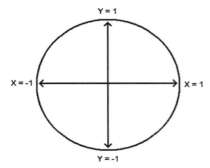

Figure 7.2
A depiction of the range of values returned by thumbstick controls.

Thumbstick Controls

Gamepads have two thumbstick controls, referred to as the left thumbstick and the right thumbstick. As depicted in Figure 7.2, these thumbsticks generate floating-point values in the range of –1 to 1 on both their X and Y coordinates when pressed by the player.

In addition to assisting you in acquiring state data for gamepad buttons, the GamePadState structure also lets you use its ThumbSticks property to retrieve data for both the left and right thumbstick controls. For example, the following statements establish a reference to a gamepad and then retrieve data from the gamepad's left thumbstick.

```
GamePadState gamePadOne = GamePad.GetState(PlayerIndex.One);
paddle.X = paddle.X + (5 * gamePadOne.ThumbSticks.Left.X);
```

The thumbpad data is used in a calculation that adjusts the location of an object named paddle by 5 pixels along the x-axis, as might be done as part of a breakout style game. Note that to reference the left thumbstick, you must specify the object representing the gamepad (gamePadOne) and then using dot notation you must specify the ThumbSticks property, followed by either Left or Right (depending upon which thumbstick you want to work with) and then X, representing the X coordinate.

Hint

Note that in this previous example, the X coordinate value returned from the left thumbstick's X coordinate is multiplied by 5 (pixels). So, if the player were pushing the thumbstick all the way to the right, X would be equal to 1 and when multiplied by 5 the result would be 5. A value of 5 is then added to the current X coordinate belonging to the paddle object, moving it 5 pixels to the right. If, on the other hand, the player was pressing the thumbstick halfway to the left, a value of .5 would be multiplied by 5, yielding a value of 2.5, which would then be added to the object's current X coordinate, moving it 2.5 pixels to the left.

The Dpad

Gamepads also have a plus-shaped Dpad control. The GamePadState object's Dpad property retrieves a structure that contains state data regarding the direction in which the gamepad's Dpad control is being pressed. The following example demonstrates how to check which direction a gamepad's Dpad is being pressed.

```
GamePadState pad1 = GamePad.GetState(PlayerIndex.One);
if (pad1.DPad.Left == ButtonState.Pressed)
{
    //Do something if the Dpad is being pressed left
}
else if (pad1.DPad.Right == ButtonState.Pressed)
{
    //Do something if the Dpad is being pressed right
}
else if (pad1.DPad.Up == ButtonState.Pressed)
{
    //Do something if the Dpad is being pressed up
}
    else if (pad1.DPad.Down == ButtonState.Pressed)
{
    //Do something if the Dpad is being pressed down
}
else
{
    //Do something if the Dpad is not being pressed
}
```

Vibrating the Gamepad

One of the additional benefits of interacting with players using gamepad controllers is that you can communicate both ways. Not only can the gamepad provide your games with player input but your games can in return provide players with feedback in the form of vibration.

Every gamepad has built-in motors that, when activated, vibrate. By turning these motors on and off, your games can let players know when certain events occur. For example, in a car racing game, your game might initiate gamepad vibration in the event the player's race car begins to drift off the track. In a shoot-up game, you might make a player's gamepad vibrate to signal when they are shot.

To make a gamepad vibrate, you need to execute the `Gamepad` class's `SetVibration()` method, as demonstrated here:

```
GamePad.SetVibration(PlayerIndex.One, 1, 1);
```

Here, the `SetVibration()` method requires that you pass it three arguments. The first argument must identify the gamepad to be affected, the second argument is a value between 0.0 and 1.0 that controls the vibration to the left motor. The third argument is a value between 0.0 and 1.0 that controls the vibration to the right motor. The lower the value passed in the second and third arguments, the weaker the vibration, and the higher the number, the stronger the vibration effect.

The previous statement makes the gamepad vibrate both its left and right motors at full strength. The following statement on the other hand, vibrates only the left motor (at half strength).

```
GamePad.SetVibration(PlayerIndex.One, .5, 0);
```

To be effective, your games need to toggle the vibration effect on and back off at the appropriate times. The following statements demonstrate how to turn off vibration.

```
GamePad.SetVibration(PlayerIndex.One, 0, 0);
```

Unless you stop vibrating a gamepad before your games ends, the gamepad will continue to vibrate. Clearly that is not desirable behavior. You must therefore take care to programmatically stop gamepad vibration before allowing your XNA games to terminate their execution. For example, if your game allows the player to terminate its execution by pressing the back button, you might control game termination by adding the following statements to your program.

```
if (GamePad.GetState(PlayerIndex.One).Buttons.Back == ButtonState.Pressed)
{
    GamePad.SetVibration(PlayerIndex.One, 0, 0);
    this.Exit();
}
```

Collecting and Processing Keyboard Input

You can use the keyboard to collect player input on both a Windows computer and the Xbox 360. To use a keyboard on the Xbox 360, simply plug a standard USB keyboard into an open Xbox 360 USB port and within a few moments, Xbox will be ready to work with it. A keyboard is a digital control and is used in games that provide the player with lots of choices that can be selected or disabled at any moment at the click of a button (e.g., key).

Different keyboards have different buttons. For example, some may have keys that control the computer's volume, while others only support a standard 101-key US key layout or perhaps a 104-key Windows layout.

Keyboard data is provided in XNA applications via the Keyboard class, which is used in conjunction with the KeyboardState structure to retrieve keyboard state data. In addition, keyboard information is made available through the Keys object and the GetPressedKeys array. The Keys object is an enumerated data type. Enumerated data types are types in which a range of name value types are available (e.g., all of the letters, numbers, and special characters available on the keyboard). The GetPressedKeys method retrieves an array made up of a list of all currently depressed keyboard keys.

Trick

One thing not included within this enumeration is uppercase keys. However, by checking to see if the Shift key is being pressed, you can determine a letter's case.

An example of how to interact with and retrieve keyboard data is provided later in this chapter.

Collecting Mouse Input

If you are creating XNA games specifically for Microsoft Windows, you have the option of the computer's mouse as an input source during game play. XNA is capable of reacting to mouse button clicks. Most mice have three digital buttons: a left button, a right button, and a mouse scroll wheel that when clicked serves as a third button. Some mice also support additional buttons on the left and right side of the mouse. The mouse scroll button also doubles as an analog control. The mouse is often used in games where the player needs to be able to select different objects. When moved, the mouse works as an analog device, providing very precise data regarding the location of the mouse pointer within the game window.

Trap

Although the Xbox supports keyboard input, it does not support use of a mouse.

A computer mouse reports data in the form of pixels, based on a coordinate system where 0,0 is the upper-left corner of the screen or window. To collect and process mouse input, you must use the Mouse class's GetState() method to

Table 7.2 XNA MouseState Properties

Property	Description
X	Horizontal coordinate of the mouse pointer.
Y	Vertical coordinate of the mouse pointer.
ScrollWheelValue	Cumulative mouse scroll wheel value.
LeftButton	State of the left mouse button.
MiddleButton	State of the middle mouse button.
RightButton	State of the right mouse button.
XButton1	State of the XBUTTON1.
XButton2	State of the XBUTTON2.

retrieve a `MouseState` object. You'll need to repeatedly execute the `GetState()` method every time the `Update()` method is executed. The `MouseState` object provides access to the current position of the mouse pointer.

The mouse pointer's location is traced via a coordinate system that originates at location 0,0, which is the upper-left corner of the game window. In this coordinate system, introduced in Chapter 5, the X coordinate represents the location of the mouse pointer along the X-axis and the Y coordinate represents the location of the mouse pointer along the Y-axis.

Hint

Pixel stands for *picture element*. A *pixel* is the smallest addressable area that can be written to or drawn on the screen or window.

Table 7.2 provides a listing of the different properties exposed through the `MouseState` object. As you can see, it provides access for up to six mouse buttons, the mouse pointer's coordinates, and the scroll wheel's value.

Trick

By default, the mouse pointer is not visible when your XNA games run on Microsoft Windows. However, you set the `Game` classes `IsMouseVisible` property to `true` to override this behavior and make it visible. To do so, all you have to do is add the following statement to the `Initialize()` method.

```
protected override void Initialize()
{
    this.IsMouseVisible = true;
    base.Initialize();
}
```

Of course, you can set `IsMouseVisible` to false to disable the display of the mouse pointer.

Interacting with Zune Users

Unlike the personal computer or Xbox, where the range of available controllers varies based on the devices that are attached, the Zune is limited to the digital and analog buttons and controllers that are built into the device. These include two digital button controls (Back and Start/Pause) and a Zune Pad, as shown in Figure 7.3.

XNA maps the Zune player's controls to gamepad controls, allowing you to interact with them using the GamePad class. Table 7.3 shows how XNA maps out the Zune player's controls to those of the gamepad.

As shown in Table 7.3, Zune's Back button is mapped to the gamepad's back button and Zune's Play/Pause button is mapped to the gamepad's B button. The Zune pad control maps to several different gamepad controls depending on how it is used. When pressed in the center as a button control, the Zune Pad maps to the gamepad's A button. When pressed on its top, bottom, left, or right sides, the Zune Pad is mapped to the gamepad's Dpad control. Lastly, any motion over the Zune Pad is mapped to the gamepad's left thumbstick.

Figure 7.3
The Zune is equipped with multiple digital controls and an analog control.

Table 7.3 Zune Controller Mapping

Zune Control	Gamepad Equivalent
Back	Back
Play/Pause	B
Zune Pad (Button)	A
Zune Pad (Dpad)	Up, Down, Left, Right
Zune Pad (Thumbstick)	Left Thumbstick

Creating Multi-Platform Games

Depending on the types of games you are creating, it is often a good idea to allow the player to control the games in different ways. For example, suppose you created a simple game that you could run on your Windows computer, Xbox 360, and Zune. If the game was complex, you might create a copy of the game for each platform and then customize each copy to support environment-specific controls.

However, if your game was not too complex, you might find it desirable to keep the programming logic for dealing with user interface controls for all three platforms together. As an example, look at the following statements.

```
GamePadState pad1 = GamePad.GetState(PlayerIndex.One);

if (pad1.Buttons.A == ButtonState.Pressed ||
    pad1.DPad.Down == ButtonState.Pressed ||
    keys.IsKeyDown(Keys.Down))
{
        //Do something
}
```

Here, logic has been added to allow the game to perform a given action using several different commands. If the game containing these statements ran on Microsoft Windows, the player could press the green A gamepad button, the downward side of the Dpad control, or the down arrow key to perform a given action. An Xbox 360 player could perform the same three actions if a keyboard is installed or just the two gamepad options if a keyboard were not available. A Zune player, on the other hand would be able to initiate that same action by the player pressing on the down side of the Zune Pad.

Creating the Control Testing Application

To bring together all of the information presented in this chapter, you will learn how to create a new XNA application called the InputCollector that demonstrates how to work with the gamepad, mouse, and keyboard. Of course, since the Zune's controls map to gamepad controls, this example can also be modified to work with Zune players. Figure 7.4 provides a view of the application in action.

As you can see, the application is organized into three sections, one section for each device type. The data retrieved from the gamepad includes data collected from the controller's Dpad, left and right thumbsticks, as well as the left and right shoulder controls. Mouse data includes the X and Y coordinate data as well as the status of the mouse's left and right buttons and wheel input. The Keyboard section displays keyboard data keyed in while the application is running. Of course, if you create a version of this application for the Zune, the only data that will be available is for the Zune controls that map to the gamepad.

In order to create this new application, you will need to perform a number of steps, as outlined here:

1. Create a new application and add a SpriteFont to it.

2. Define game world data.

3. Set up application initialization.

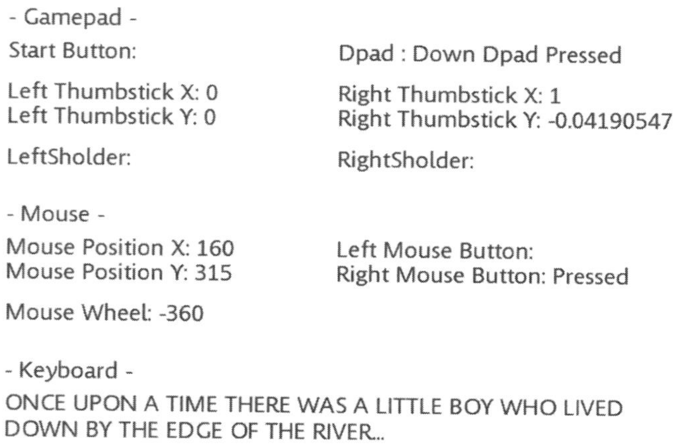

- Gamepad -

Start Button: Dpad : Down Dpad Pressed

Left Thumbstick X: 0   Right Thumbstick X: 1
Left Thumbstick Y: 0   Right Thumbstick Y: -0.04190547

LeftSholder: RightSholder:

- Mouse -

Mouse Position X: 160   Left Mouse Button:
Mouse Position Y: 315   Right Mouse Button: Pressed

Mouse Wheel: -360

- Keyboard -

ONCE UPON A TIME THERE WAS A LITTLE BOY WHO LIVED
DOWN BY THE EDGE OF THE RIVER...

Figure 7.4
An example of the InputCollector application in action.

4. Modify the Update() method to collect and process user input.

5. Modify the Draw() method to display application output.

Once you have completed all of these steps, you will be able to save and run the application on your computer. Later, in Chapter 11, you will learn how to modify and port your application over to other platforms, including the Zune and Xbox 360.

Adding a SpriteFont to Display Test Output

The first step in creating this new application is to create a new project and then add a SpriteFont to it in order to enable the application to display text. The following procedures outline the steps involved in performing this task.

1. Click on File > New Project and then select Windows Game (3.1). Name the project InputCollector and then click on OK.

2. Add a SpriteFont to the application by going into Solution Explorer, right-clicking on Content, and then clicking on Add > New Item. The Add new Item – Content window appears, as shown in Figure 7.5.

3. Select the SpriteFont icon and click on Add. XNA will add a SpriteFont named SpriteFont1.spritefont to the project.

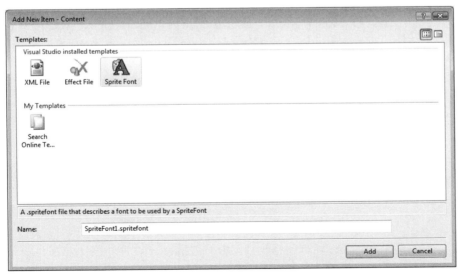

Figure 7.5
Adding a SpriteFont to the application.

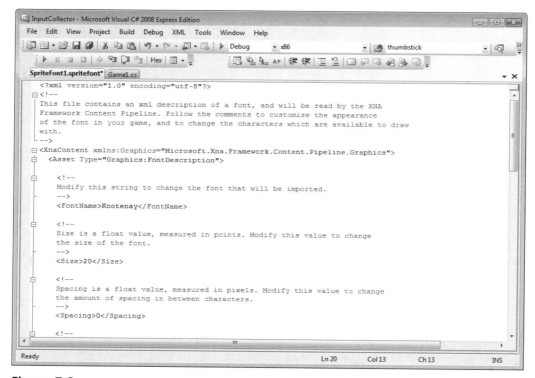

Figure 7.6
Editing the SpriteFont file in order to change font size.

4. The SpriteFont file is an XML file. Once added, the files are displayed in the code editor. Modify this file by changing its default font size from 14 to 20 (e.g., overtype the value specified in between the <Size> and </Size> tags) as shown in Figure 7.6.

5. Close the SpriteFont1.spritefont file.

6. Now that you added the SpriteFont to the application, you need to add the program required to load and use the font within the application. To do so, begin by defining a SpriteFont variable named font as part of the game world data (place the declaration statement at the beginning of the C# program as one of the first statements in the Game1 class).

```
public class Game1 : Microsoft.Xna.Framework.Game
{
    GraphicsDeviceManager graphics;
    SpriteBatch spriteBatch;
```

```
SpriteFont font;  //Declare variable to store font
     .
     .
     .
```

7. Now that you have defined the `font` variable, you can use it to set up a reference to the `SpriteFont` that you just added to the application. To do so, add the following statements to the beginning of the `LoadContent()` method.

```
//Load the font used to display windows text
font = Content.Load<SpriteFont>("SpriteFont1");
```

Now that you have created your new application and added and configured the use of a `SpriteFont`, you are ready to begin assembling the program logic required to make your new application work.

Defining Game World Data

The second step in the creation of the InputCollector application is the definition of a number of variables and an array for storing various types of game world (application) data. *Game world* data is data that is universally accessible throughout the application. To facilitate this, the code statements that make up the game data, shown below, must be placed at the beginning of the application in the game class (but not within any of the class's methods).

```
public class Game1 : Microsoft.Xna.Framework.Game
{
    GraphicsDeviceManager graphics;
    SpriteBatch spriteBatch;

    SpriteFont font;  //Declare variable to store font
    Color ScreenColor = Color.White;  //Define background color

    //Declare variables used to collect and report gamepad data
    String StartMsg = "";
    String DpadMsg = "";
    String LThumbX = "";
    String LThumbY = "";
    String RThumbX = "";
    String RThumbY = "";
    String LShoulder = "";
    String RShoulder = "";
```

```
//Declare variables used to collect and report keyboard data
String mouseX = "";
String mouseY = "";
String LMouse = "";
String RMouse = "";
String MouseWheel = "";

//Declare variable and array used to collect and report mouse data
String KeyboardText = "";
Keys[] PrevKeyPresses = new Keys[0];
    .
    .
    .
```

The game world data used by this application includes the SpriteFont variable, which you have already added to the application, as well as three other different sets of data. The first set is a collection of eight variables that will be used to collect and report gamepad data. Each of these variables is descriptively named, allowing you to identify the type of gamepad input that it will store. The second set of data is a series of five variables that will store data collected from the mouse. Again, each variable's name identifies the type of data it stores. The third set of data consists of a string variable that will be used to store any keyboard input typed in by the user as well as an array named PrevKeyPresses, which will be used to keep track of user input in order to help the application identify when something new has been keyed in. In addition, a value of Color.White has been assigned to the default ScreenColor variable, defining the application's background color.

Application Initialization

The third step in the development of your new application is to modify the Initialize() method for the purpose of making the mouse pointer visible within the application window when the application runs. By default, XNA hides the mouse pointer. To make it visible, you must set the Game1 class's IsMouse-Visible property equal to true, as shown here:

```
protected override void Initialize()
{
    this.IsMouseVisible = true;
    base.Initialize();
}
```

Trick

> C# supports the use of the `this` keyword. `this` references the current object, which in the case of the `Initialize()` method is a reference to the `Game1` class.

Keeping the Game Updated

The fourth step in the development of your new application is to add the programming logic that is responsible for interacting with all the computer's input devices and processing all the input. This programming logic will have to be repeatedly executed in order to capture every thumbstick movement, every button push, every keystroke, and so on. Therefore, this programming logic belongs in the `Update()` method.

To help keep things simple, you will add the programming code that goes in the `Update()` method in a series of steps, as outlined here:

1. Retrieve input device state data.

2. Manage application termination.

3. Add program code to capture gamepad input.

4. Add program code to capture mouse input.

5. Add program code to capture keyboard input.

Retrieving Input Device State Data

Let's begin by modifying the `Update()` method to define three variables that will be used to store state data each time the `Update()` method runs. The data collected will be captured from the gamepad, mouse, and keyboard.

```
protected override void Update(GameTime gameTime)
{
    //Retrieve gamepad, keyboard and mouse state data
    GamePadState pad1 = GamePad.GetState(PlayerIndex.One);
    KeyboardState keys = Keyboard.GetState();
    MouseState MouseObj = Mouse.GetState();

    // Allows the game to exit
    if (GamePad.GetState(PlayerIndex.One).Buttons.Back ==
      ButtonState.Pressed)
        this.Exit();
```

```
    base.Update(gameTime);

}
```

As you can see, game state data is retrieved using the GetState() method and stored in descriptive variables.

Managing Application Termination

Next, let's modify the statement in the Update() method that managed game termination. This change will allow the user to respond and terminate application execution in a number of different ways.

```
// Allows the game to exit
if (GamePad.GetState(PlayerIndex.One).Buttons.Back ==
    ButtonState.Pressed || keys.IsKeyDown(Keys.Escape))
    this.Exit();
```

As you can see, this statement now allows the game to be terminated by either pressing the gamepad's Back button or the keyboard's Escape key.

Interacting with the Gamepad

The next set of statements need to be added to the end of the Update() method and will be used to manage interaction with the various controls that make up the gamepad controller.

```
//Process gamepad buttons (A, B, X, and Y)
if (pad1.Buttons.A == ButtonState.Pressed) ScreenColor = Color.LightGreen;
if (pad1.Buttons.B == ButtonState.Pressed) ScreenColor = Color.IndianRed;
if (pad1.Buttons.X == ButtonState.Pressed) ScreenColor = Color.LightBlue;
if (pad1.Buttons.Y == ButtonState.Pressed) ScreenColor = Color.Yellow;
```

These four statements turn the console window's background color to one of four different colors, depending on whether the gamepad's A, B, X, or Y button is pressed. Next, add the following statements to the Update() method.

```
//Process gamepad Start button
if (pad1.Buttons.Start == ButtonState.Pressed) {
    StartMsg = "Pressed";
}
else
{
    StartMsg = "";
```

```
}

//Process gamepad DPad input
if (pad1.DPad.Left == ButtonState.Pressed)
{
    DpadMsg = "Left DPad Pressed";
}
    else if (pad1.DPad.Right == ButtonState.Pressed)
{
    DpadMsg = "Right DPad Pressed";
}
    else if (pad1.DPad.Up == ButtonState.Pressed)
{
    DpadMsg = "Up DPad Pressed";
}
    else if (pad1.DPad.Down == ButtonState.Pressed)
{
    DpadMsg = "Down Dpad Pressed";
}
    else
{
    DpadMsg = "";
}
```

The first set of statements react when the gamepad's Start button is pressed, assigning a value of "Pressed" to StartMsg. If the Start button is not being pressed, an empty string is assigned to StartMsg. Next, an if statement code block is set up to process Dpad input, assigning different text strings whenever the user presses one of its four sides. Next, add the following statements to the Update() method.

```
//Process gamepad left and right thumbstick input
LThumbX = pad1.ThumbSticks.Left.X.ToString();
LThumbY = pad1.ThumbSticks.Left.Y.ToString();
RThumbX = pad1.ThumbSticks.Right.X.ToString();
RThumbY = pad1.ThumbSticks.Right.Y.ToString();
```

These statements capture and process input from the gamepad's two thumb-sticks. The data supplied by each thumbstick control is converted to a string using the ToString() method. This will allow the data to be displayed when referenced later in the Draw() method. Next, add the following statement to the Update() method.

```
//Process gamepad left and right shoulder buttons
if (pad1.Buttons.LeftShoulder == ButtonState.Pressed)
{
    LShoulder = "Pressed";
}
else
{
    LShoulder = "";
}
    if (pad1.Buttons.RightShoulder == ButtonState.Pressed)
{
    RShoulder = "Pressed";
}
else
{
    RShoulder = "";
}
```

As you can see, these statements process input for the gamepad's right and left shoulder buttons, assigning different text string values to the RShoulder and LShoulder variables depending on whether the buttons are being pressed.

Collecting and Reporting Mouse Data

Now it is time to start collecting mouse data. To do so, add the following statements to the Update() method.

```
//Store mouse pointer coordinates
mouseX = MouseObj.X.ToString();
mouseY = MouseObj.Y.ToString();
```

These statements retrieve the mouse pointer's X and Y coordinates within the application window and then convert that data into a string. Next, add the following statements to the Update() method.

```
//Process left and right mouse buttons
if (MouseObj.LeftButton == ButtonState.Pressed)
{
    LMouse = "Pressed";
}
else
{
    LMouse = "";
```

```
}

if (MouseObj.RightButton == ButtonState.Pressed)
{
    RMouse = "Pressed";
}
else
{
    RMouse = "";
}
```

These statements determine if the left and right mouse buttons have been pressed and display text strings indicating the current state. To capture mouse wheel data, add the following statements to the Update() method.

```
//Process Mouse wheel data
MouseWheel = MouseObj.ScrollWheelValue.ToString();
```

Here, mouse wheel data is retrieved using the ScrollWheelValue property, converted to a string value and assigned to a variable named MouseWheel.

Processing Keyboard Input

Now it's time to tackle the collection and processing of keyboard input. Specifically, you will add program code designed to intercept key presses, allowing keyboard input to be dynamically displayed on the console window as it's keyed in. Begin by adding the following statements to the Update() method.

```
//Define an array and load it with a list of pressed keys
Keys[] CurrentKeys;
CurrentKeys = keys.GetPressedKeys();
```

Next, an array named CurrentKeys is defined and populated with keyboard data using the GetPressedKeys() method. Next, add the following statements to the end of the Update() method.

```
//Process keyboard input and store as a string
for (int i = 0; i < CurrentKeys.Length; i++)
{
    bool match = false;
    for (int j = 0; j < PrevKeyPresses.Length; j++)
    {
        if (CurrentKeys[i] == PrevKeyPresses[j])
        {
```

```
                    match = true;
                    break;
                }
            }
            if (match == false)
            {
                switch (CurrentKeys[i])
                {
                    case Keys.Space:
                        KeyboardText = KeyboardText + " ";
                        break;
                    case Keys.Enter:
                        KeyboardText = KeyboardText + "\n";
                        break;
                    case Keys.OemPeriod:
                        KeyboardText = KeyboardText + ".";
                        break;
                    default:
                        KeyboardText = KeyboardText + CurrentKeys[i].ToString();
                        break;
                }
            }
        }
    }
}
PrevKeyPresses = CurrentKeys;
```

Here, a for loop has been set up to process the CurrentKeys array. This loop
iterates once for each item in the array. Within the loop, a second for loop is used
to iterate through the PrevKeyPresses array. Within this loop, an if statement
code block has been set up for the purpose of determining if the current item
(character) in the CurrentKeys array is the same as the current item (character)
in the PrevKeyPresses array. If a match occurs, the for loop terminates its
processing.

If new keyboard input was found (i.e., the user typed in something not previously
processed), a switch code bock is executed. The reason behind the switch code
block is that some keyboard input requires additional translation before it can be
displayed. The first case statement is used to add a blank space to the end of the
text string stored in the KeyboardText variable. The second case statement adds
the \n (newline) characters to the end of the text string whenever the Enter key is
pressed. The third case statement adds a period (.) to the end of the text string.
The switch code block's default option assigns any other keyboard input to the

end of the text string stored in the KeyboardText variable after converting it to a string. The last statement shown above updates the value of PrevKeyPresses by assigning it the value stored in CurrentKeys.

Hint

As shown in Table 7.4, most keystrokes generate output that you would expect. For example, if the A key is pressed a value of A is generated. However, some keystrokes generate non-intuitive results. For example, if the space key is pressed, a string value of Space is returned instead of a single blank space. The purpose of the switch code block in the Update() method is to convert several keyboard values into a more appropriate format for the application. However, as Table 7.4 shows, there are many unaccounted for keystroke values in the application.

Displaying Output

The fifth and final step in the creation of the InputCollection application is to modify the Draw() method to provide for the display of gamepad, mouse, and keyboard data. To do so, you will have to define Vector2 objects that specify the coordinate location for all output text, which it organizes and displays in three primary sections on the window console.

```
protected override void Draw(GameTime gameTime)
{
    GraphicsDevice.Clear(ScreenColor);

    Color Pur = Color.Purple;   //Define text color for headings
    Color Blu = Color.Blue;     //Define text color for detailed data

    //Specify the coordinates where console text is to be written
    Vector2 v1 = new Vector2(20, 10);    //Gamepad------
    Vector2 v2 = new Vector2(20, 50);    //Start Button
    Vector2 v3 = new Vector2(410, 50);   //Dpad
    Vector2 v4 = new Vector2(20, 100);   //Left Thumbstick X
    Vector2 v5 = new Vector2(20, 130);   //Left Thumbstick Y
    Vector2 v6 = new Vector2(410, 100);  //Right Thumbstick X
    Vector2 v7 = new Vector2(410, 130);  //Right Thumbstick Y
    Vector2 v8 = new Vector2(20, 180);   //Left Shoulder
    Vector2 v9 = new Vector2(410, 180);  //Right Shoulder
    Vector2 v10 = new Vector2(20, 250);  //Mouse------
    Vector2 v11 = new Vector2(20, 290);  //Mouse X Coordinate
    Vector2 v12 = new Vector2(20, 320);  //Mouse Y Coordinate
    Vector2 v13 = new Vector2(410, 290); //Mouse Left Button
    Vector2 v14 = new Vector2(410, 320); //Mouse Right Button
    Vector2 v15 = new Vector2(20, 370);  //Mouse Wheel
```

Table 7.4 Keyboard Key Enumerations

Key	Description	Key	Description	Key	Description
A	A key	F21	F21 key	OemBacklash	Oem angle key
Add	Add key	F22	F22 key	OemClear	CLEAR key
Apps	Applications key	F23	F23 key	OemCloseBrackets	OEM Close bracket key
Attn	Attn key	F24	F24 key	OemComma	Country "," key
B	B key	F3	F3 key	OemCopy	OEM Copy key
Back	BACKSPACE key	F4	F4 key	OemEnIW	OEM Enlarge Window key
BrowserBack	Browser Back key	F5	F5 key	OemMinus	Country "-" key
BrowserFavorites	Browser Favorites key	F6	F6 key	OemOpenBrackets	OEM open bracket key
BrowserForward	Browser Forward key	F7	F7 key	OemPeriod	Country "." key
BrowserHome	Browser Start/Home key	F8	F8 key	OEMPipe	OEM pipe key
BrowserRefresh	Browser Refresh key	F9	F9 key	OEMPlus	Country "+" key
BrowserSearch	Browser Search key	G	G key	OEMQuestion	OEM question mark key
BrowserStop	Browser Stop key	H	H key	OEMQuotes	OEM Quote key
C	C key	Help	HELP key	OEMSemicolon	OEM Semicolon key
CapsLock	CAPS LOCK key	Home	HOME key	OEMTilde	Oem tilde key
ChatPadGreen	Green ChatPad key	I	I key	P	P key
ChatPadOrange	Orange ChatPad key	ImeConvert	IME Convert key	Pa1	PA1 key
Crsel	CrSel key	ImeNoCovert	IME NoConvert key	PageDown	PAGE DOWN key
D	D key	Insert	INS key	PageUp	PAGE UP key
D0	Varying characters	J	J key	Pause	PAUSE key
D1	Varying characters	K	K key	Play	PLAY key
D2	Varying characters	Kana	Kana key (Japanese)	Print	PRINT key
D3	Varying characters	Kanji	Janji key (Japanese)	PrintScreen	PRINT SCREEN key
D4	Varying characters	L	L key	ProcessKey	IME PROCESS key
D5	Varying characters	LaunchApplication1	Start Application 1	Q	Q key

D6	Varying characters	LaunchApplication2	Start Application 2	R	R key
D7	Varying characters	LaunchMail	Start mail key	Right	RIGHT ARROW key
D8	Varying characters	Left	LEFT arrow key	RightAlt	Right ALT key
D9	Varying characters	LeftAlt	Left ALT key	RightControl	Right CONTROL key
Decimal	Decimal key	LeftControl	Left CONTROL key	RightShift	Right SHIFT key
Delete	DEL key	LeftShift	Left Shift key	RightWindows	Right Windows key
Divide	Divide key	LeftWindows	Left Windows key	S	S key
Down	DOWN ARROW key	M	M key	Scroll	SCROLL LOCK key
E	E key	MediaNextTrack	Next Track key	Select	SELECT key
End	END key	MediaPlayPause	Play/Pause key	SelectMedia	Select media key
Enter	ENTER key	MediaPreviousTrack	Previous Track key	Separator	Separator key
EraseEof	Erase EOF key	MediaStop	Stop key	Sleep	Sleep key
Escape	ESC key	Multiply	Multiply key	Space	SPACEBAR
Execute	EXECUTE key	N	N key	Subtract	Subtract key
Exsel	ExSel key	None	Reserved	T	T key
F	F key	NumLock	NUM LOCK key	Tab	TAB key
F1	F1 key	NumPad0	0 key	U	U key
F10	F10 key	NumPad1	1 key	Up	UP ARROW key
F11	F11 key	NumPad2	2 key	V	V key
F12	F12 key	NumPad3	3 key	VolumeDown	Volume Down key
F13	F13 key	NumPad4	4 key	VolumeMute	Volume Mute key
F14	F14 key	NumPad5	5 key	VolumeUp	Volume Up key
F15	F15 key	NumPad6	6 key	W	W key
F16	F16 key	NumPad7	7 key	X	X key
F17	F17 key	NumPad8	8 key	Y	Y key
F18	F18 key	NumPad9	9 key	Z	Z key
F19	F19 key	0	0 key	Zoom	Zoom key
F2	F2 key	Oem8	Varying characters		
F20	F20 key	OemAuto	OEM Auto key		

```
Vector2 v16 = new Vector2(20, 440);  //Keyboard- - - - - - -
Vector2 v17 = new Vector2(20, 480);  //Typing area

spriteBatch.Begin();
spriteBatch.DrawString(font, "- Gamepad -", v1, Pur);
spriteBatch.DrawString(font, "Start Button: " + StartMsg, v2, Blu);
spriteBatch.DrawString(font, "Dpad : " + DpadMsg, v3, Blu);
spriteBatch.DrawString(font, "Left Thumbstick X: " + LThumbX, v4, Blu);
spriteBatch.DrawString(font, "Left Thumbstick Y: " + LThumbY, v5, Blu);
spriteBatch.DrawString(font, "Right Thumbstick X: " + RThumbX, v6, Blu);
spriteBatch.DrawString(font, "Right Thumbstick Y: " + RThumbY, v7, Blu);
spriteBatch.DrawString(font, "LeftShoulder: " + LShoulder, v8, Blu);
spriteBatch.DrawString(font, "RightShoulder: " + RShoulder, v9, Blu);
spriteBatch.DrawString(font, "- Mouse -", v10, Pur);
spriteBatch.DrawString(font, "Mouse Position X: " + mouseX, v11, Blu);
spriteBatch.DrawString(font, "Mouse Position Y: " + mouseY, v12, Blu);
spriteBatch.DrawString(font, "Left Mouse Button: " + LMouse, v13, Blu);
spriteBatch.DrawString(font, "Right Mouse Button: " + RMouse, v14, Blu);
spriteBatch.DrawString(font, "Mouse Wheel: " + MouseWheel, v15, Blu);
spriteBatch.DrawString(font, "- Keyboard -", v16, Pur);
spriteBatch.DrawString(font, KeyboardText, v17, Blu);
spriteBatch.End();

base.Draw(gameTime);
}
```

As you can see, the first statement in this method sets the application's window to the background color specified in the ScreenColor variable. Next, two variables named Pur and Blu are defined and assigned a color value. These variables are used in the statements that follow to specify the color of output text.

The next set of statements creates a series of Vector2 objects, assigning them various coordinates on the console window. These Vector2 objects are then used in the final set of statements to display the application's output on the console window. Output is drawn using the DrawString() method. Each time a new line of text is drawn, the SpriteFont assigned to the font variable is used to specify the text and variable data that is displayed.

Once you have updated the Draw() method, your new application should be ready for execution. Assuming you followed along carefully and did not skip any steps or make any typos, everything should work as expected.

Hint

Don't forget that the source code for this application is available for download from the book's companion web page (www.courseptr.com/downloads).

Summary

In this chapter, you learned how to work with various input devices including the gamepad, keyboard, and mouse. You also learned how the Zune player's controls map to gamepad controls, allowing your applications to interact with them using the same program code that works with gamepad controllers. Using the information provided in this chapter, you will be able to develop games that can be played using one or more of the controllers covered in this chapter.

CHAPTER 8

WORKING WITH IMAGES

Modern computer games are very graphical. They include a bevy of different graphics and backgrounds on which graphics are displayed and moved about. This chapter will show you how to add graphics to your XNA applications and how to display them on the screen. You will learn how to build an electronic picture viewer application and will lay the foundation you will need in Chapters 10 and 11 to create arcade-style computer games.

An overview of the major topics covered in this chapter includes learning:

- How to add graphics to your XNA games

- About the different graphic formats supported by XNA

- How to control the size of graphics

- How to specify the placement of graphics in the game window

Graphics Can Make or Break Your Games

One of the first things players notice when playing a new game is the quality of the game's graphics. Dull or poorly drawn graphics may drive away some players before they even give your games a chance. The creation of graphics for computer games is not a simple endeavor. Graphic design is a complicated process that requires advanced software and considerable artistic skills.

It you have good artistic skills, then you should be good to go. If not, perhaps you know someone with a knack for graphic development and can partner with that person when developing your computer games. If this is not the case, you'll find plenty of sources of quality graphics available on the internet. Some are free and some can be purchased. When acquiring graphics over the internet, be sure you comply with any copyright restrictions the creator may impose.

As important as graphics are to the overall experience of playing computer games, it is fair to say that you can easily create some very cool and very popular games using only the simplest graphics. Take Tetris-style games as an example. Their graphics are colorful but simple and yet these games have become enormously popular.

Great graphics are no guarantee of success. There are plenty of eye-popping games that nobody wants to play. All the graphics in the world won't make a poorly designed game fun to play.

Adding Graphics to Your XNA Games

XNA allows you to draw graphic images that you supply on the game window. As with drawing text, the drawing of graphics involves the placement of graphic images in the game window based on a coordinate system whose origin begins at the upper-left corner (0,0). This coordinate system is based on pixels. A *pixel* is the smallest addressable location on the game window.

Trap

It is important to keep a close eye on the size of your graphics files. While XNA will automatically scale them as specified within your applications, using graphics that are larger than you need them to be requires the excess use of system memory, which can have a direct impact on the performance of your applications. Since the Xbox and most personal computers have plenty of memory, this issue is somewhat mitigated. However, the Zune player has limited memory. In addition, the Zune player is limited to a maximum display size of 320×240 pixels. Any XNA games that you generate for the Zune Player will benefit from the use of graphics smaller than 320×240.

XNA works with a wide range of graphic file formats, each of which has its own specific set of properties. Graphic file formats are identified by their assigned three or four character file extension. For example, Portable Network Graphics (.png) files can be used to store images with lots of detail. PNG files also support transparency, which is most useful in games where graphics move about and interact with one another. Table 8.1 lists and describes all of the different graphics file types that XNA supports.

Table 8.1 XNA Supported Graphic File Types

File Type	Description
.bmp	Bitmap files are uncompressed graphic files that tend to be relatively large compared to other graphic formats.
.jpg/.jpeg	Joint Photographic Experts Group files are compressed files commonly used to store photographs. It is best used for images with fewer than 256 colors but which require great detail.
.dib	Device-independent bitmap files are a variation of BMP files.
.dds	DirectDraw Surface files are DirectX graphic files designed to work with DirectX and feature transparency.
.hdr	High Dynamic Range files are used to store high-quality photographs requiring high levels of detail.
.pfm	A bitmap file type developed by Adobe.
.png	Portable Network Graphics files are compressed graphic files best used for photos and other graphics files that contain a large range of colors. PNG files are generally preferred by XNA developers because of its support for lossless graphics and transparency.
.ppm	Portable Pixel Map files are bitmap files supported by various graphic editor programs.
.tga	Targa files are similar to PNG files but support less color depth.

Managing Game Content

XNA games involve the use of many different types of content, including fonts, graphics, and audio. These types of contents are often referred to as *assets*. Although it has not been highlighted up to this point in this book, assets are added to your XNA projects and managed through a mechanism referred to as the *content pipeline*. The content pipeline is responsible for taking the content you supply and converting it to an internal format that XNA can work with.

Once added to the content pipeline, XNA manages all project content for you, alleviating you of any concerns about differences in the types of files you may have added to your projects. As such you can, for example, create XNA games that use JPEG, PNG, and BMP graphic files without having to worry about the format of each individual file.

To verify that an asset has been recognized by XNA, expand the content folder in the Solution Explorer window and select the asset. Properties for the selected asset are then displayed in the Properties window (click on View > Properties Window if that window is not currently open). For example, Figure 8.3 shows the properties belonging to a graphic file named ball.png. The asset name that XNA

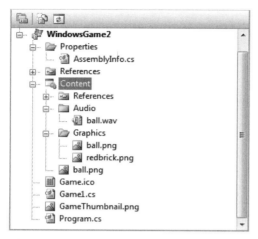

Figure 8.1
The Graphics folder contains three graphic files.

automatically creates for this file is ball (e.g., the filename less its file extension). Seeing data populated in the Properties window for a graphic file is an indication that XNA is able to work with it and that you will not get any compile errors as a result of adding the graphic file to your XNA project.

Trap

Assets must be uniquely named within the Content folder in order to prevent an error from occurring. However, you can add subfolders to the Content folder in order to further organize your application's assets, creating, for example, separate subfolders for graphics and audio files. In doing so, your application can support assets with duplication names. To add a new subfolder to the Content folder, right-click on the Content folder and select Add > New Folder. Figure 8.1 shows an example where two subfolders have been added to the application. Note that the Audio folder contains a file named ball.wav and the Graphics folder contains files named ball.png and redbrick.png, resulting in duplication asset names (e.g., two instances of ball), which is okay since they are maintained in different folders.

Adding Graphic Content to Your XNA Projects

You add graphic files to your applications via the content pipeline in much the same way that you add other types of content (including fonts). The first step in incorporating the use of graphics into your XNA games is to import them into your XNA projects. This is done by right-clicking on the Content element located in the Solution Explorer window and then selecting Add > Existing Item option as shown in Figure 8.2.

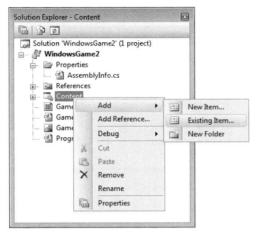

Figure 8.2
Adding a new graphic asset to an XNA project.

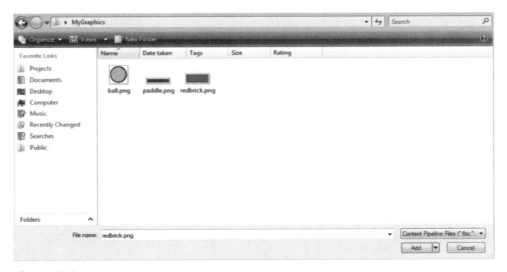

Figure 8.3
To finish adding the graphic file, select it and click on Add.

The Add Existing Item – Content window then appears, as shown in Figure 8.3. Using this window you can select the graphic file that you want to import into the application.

Using this simple set of steps you can add any number of the various types of graphic file types listed in Table 8.1 to your XNA projects.

Trick

XNA makes copies of any resources you add to your projects and places them in its Content folder (e.g., in Solution Explorer). If you want to use the same resource in several XNA applications, you can optionally add a link to the resource. To do so, right-click on the Content folder and click on Add > Existing Item and then click on the down arrow located on the right-hand side of the Add button and then select the Add As Link option as shown in Figure 8.4.

A big advantage of using this option is that it allows you to modify a resource external to your XNA projects and then to incorporate the modified resource into your XNA applications the next time you compile them.

Defining Variables for Your Assets

Once you have imported the graphic files your XNA game requires and the XNA content pipeline has generated an asset name for each file, you can begin making use of them within the application. In order to be able to programmatically interact with and control the use of graphics in your XNA games, you must define and associate a unique variable for each asset. For example, the following statement defines a variable named gameBall.

```
Texture2D gameBall;
```

In XNA, the graphic images that are drawn are referred to as textures. These textures are drawn on top of 2D or 3D models. In the case of the examples

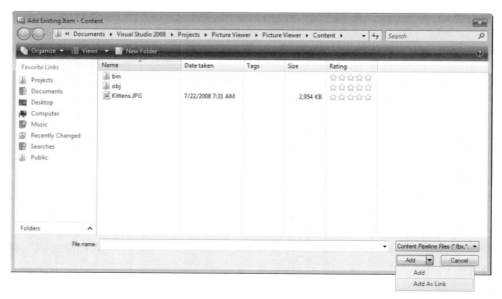

Figure 8.4
XNA will follow the link to the resource when your XNA application is compiled.

presented in this book, you'll be working with a 2D model of type Texture2D. This data type manipulates two-dimensional graphics, drawing them on a flat surface area of the screen. Note that as is the case when defining any variable, you must specify the type of variable being defined. In the case of the gameBall variable, a type of Texture2D has been specified. Texture2D is a 2D image that is applied to an object.

Hint

Texture2D is just one of many different types of textures supported by XNA. Other types of textures support the application of images on top of different types of 3D models.

Loading Game Assets

Once you have loaded content into the content pipeline and then defined variables with which to reference them, you can load the assets, allowing you to programmatically work with them. To load an asset, you must use the Content property as shown below. The property belongs to the ContentManager class. The Content property provides access to any asset in the content pipeline. The ContentManager also supports the Load method, which provides the ability to load any asset that has been defined within your game.

```
gameBall = Content.Load<Texture2D>(@"Graphics\ball");
```

The Load method is a generic method that can be used to load any asset. As such, you can use the method to retrieve and load any type of content resource that you add to your XNA application, be it a 2D or a 3D graphic or an audio file. In order to work, you must tell the method the type of resource being loaded. Note the specification of the @ character, which instructs XNA to process the path string that follows exactly as shown, beginning in the Content folder.

Hint

In the previous example, it was assumed that the ball asset had been defined within the Graphics subfolder located within the Content folder. If the ball asset were instead defined directly within the Content folder, then the following statement would need to be used to load the asset.

```
gameBall = Content.Load<Texture2D>(@"ball");
```

Using the Rectangle Structure to Manage the Placement of Graphics

When you load and manipulate graphics into your games, the graphics are often referred to by game developers as sprites. A *sprite* then is a preloaded graphic file displayed and moved about the screen during game play. In order to control the placement and movement of sprites on the screen, you can use the `Rectangle` structure.

The `Rectangle` structure is used to store coordinate and size location for the rectangle (and therefore for its contents). To define a `Rectangle`, you must adhere to the following syntax.

`variableName = new Rectangle(x, y, width, height);`

Here, *x* and *y* represent coordinate values and *width* and *height* specify the size of the graphic in pixels. Figure 8.5 depicts the relationship of these four arguments to the placement of the sprite on the game window.

Working with Assets

Now that you have defined a local variable with which to set up a reference to a graphic image, have loaded it into memory, and have created a rectangle with which to control its placement, you are ready to display it on the screen. To do so, you need to draw it, which you can do using the `SpriteBatch` class. The `SpriteBatch` class provides you with access to methods that allow you to begin, end, and perform draw operations.

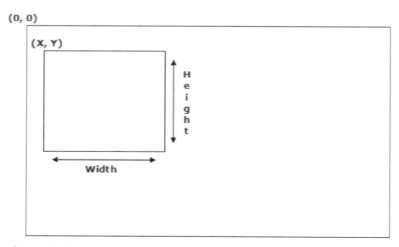

Figure 8.5
You can use the `Rectangle` structure to control the placement of your sprites.

Hint

To make things easy, XNA automatically defines a `SpriteBatch` variable for you in the `LoadContent` method of every new XNA project, as shown here.

```
protected override void LoadContent()
{
    //Create a new SpriteBatch, which can be used to draw textures.
    spriteBatch = new SpriteBatch(GraphicsDevice);
}
```

Note that the variable declared here begins with a lowercase character (e.g., `spriteBatch`) whereas the reference to the `SpriteBatch` class begins with a capital letter.

Drawing operations should occur with the XNA application's `Draw` method. Before you can begin drawing, you must execute the `SpriteBatch` class's `Begin` method, as shown here.

```
spriteBatch.Begin();
```

You can then use the `SpriteBatch` class's `Draw` method to draw on the screen. The `Draw` method has the following syntax.

```
spriteBatch.Draw(Texture, Position, Color);
```

The `draw` method accepts three arguments. *Texture* identifies the name of a `Texture2D` variable that specifies the graphic image to be drawn. *Position* specifies the coordinate location at which the graphic image is to be drawn. *Color* specifies the tinting color to be applied to (or shined on) the graphic image.

When done drawing, you must execute the `SpriteBatch` class's `End` method, as demonstrated here.

```
spriteBatch.End();
```

Bringing It All Together

Okay, let's put together everything you have learned so far into an example application that displays a picture on the game window. Begin by creating a new XNA project named `DisplayingGraphics`. Since this application will display a picture, you will need a graphic file. If you do not have one, you can download a copy of the kittens.jpg file along with the source code for this project from the book's companion web page located at www.courseptr.com/downloads/.

Once you have a graphic file, add it to your new application. At this point you are ready to begin the coding process. Start by adding the following variable declaration statements to your program, shown below in bold. These statements represent game world data and as such should be placed at the beginning of the program, at the start of the Game1 class definition, outside of any of the program's methods. This will make the variables globally accessible throughout the program.

```
public class Game1 : Microsoft.Xna.Framework.Game
{
    GraphicsDeviceManager graphics;
    SpriteBatch spriteBatch;

    //Define a texture variable to be used to display a graphic
    Texture2D Kittens;

    //Define rectangle with which to display graphics
    Rectangle DisplayRect;
        .
        .
        .
```

As you can see, the first variable declaration specifies a variable named Kittens as a Texture2D type. This variable will be used to load and reference the graphic file named kittens.jpg later in the program. The second variable is named Display-Rect. It is of type rectangle and will be used to specify the size and location at which the graphic is displayed on the application window.

Now that you have defined global variables representing a graphic and a rectangle, which the application will use to manage the display of its picture, you need to create an instance of a rectangle object within your program. The best place to do this is within the Initialize() method, as shown below. The Initialize() method is the first method that the program executes when it starts. This will ensure its immediate availability in the program.

```
protected override void Initialize()
{
    //Instantiate the rectangle
    DisplayRect = new Rectangle(0, 0, 640, 480);

    base.Initialize();
}
```

Here, a Rectangle object has been instantiated. The arguments passed to the Rectangle() method instruct XNA to place the rectangle at coordinates 0,0 (the upper-left hand corner of the application window) and to make it 640 pixels wide by 480 pixels high. The newly created Rectangle is then assigned to the DisplayRect variable, providing you with a means of referring to it in the program.

Now you are ready to load a copy of the kittens.jpg file into memory. To do so, you must use the ContentManager class's Content property and Load method, as shown here:

```
protected override void LoadContent()
{
    //Create a new SpriteBatch, which can be used to draw textures.
    spriteBatch = new SpriteBatch(GraphicsDevice);

    //Load the specified graphic file
    Kittens = Content.Load<Texture2D>(@"Kittens");
}
```

As you can see, the LoadContent() method has been chosen as the best place in which to load the graphic into memory, which makes perfect sense because the LoadContent() method's job is to load the resources required by the game.

The last step in the development of the DisplayingGraphics application is to perform the actual drawing of the graphic on the application window. To facilitate this, you need to add a little program code to the Draw() method, as shown here:

Hint

Because this application is small and performs a single action (i.e., displaying a picture) you do not need to place any code of your own in the Update() method. However, 99.9% of the time, you'll find that the Update() method is the central location within your C# program where all the program's high-level controlling logic is placed.

```
protected override void Draw(GameTime gameTime)
{
    GraphicsDevice.Clear(Color.White);

    //Draw the currently specified picture on the application window
    spriteBatch.Begin();
    spriteBatch.Draw(Kittens, DisplayRect, Color.White);
    spriteBatch.End();

    base.Draw(gameTime);
}
```

Figure 8.6
By default XNA displays the picture starting at the upper-left corner of the window.

As you can see, the SpriteBatch class's Draw method, embedded within the class's Begin and End method, is used to draw the graphic on the application window. Note that the Draw method is passed three arguments, specifying the variable name of the graphic, the variable name of the Rectangle within which the graphic will be shown, and the color to be applied to the image. Figure 8.6 shows an example of how the application looks when run.

Creating a Picture Viewer

The DisplayGraphics application displays its graphic at actual size starting in the upper-left corner of the screen. If the graphic is smaller than the screen size, then the picture ends up displaying on a color background, as is the case of the example shown in Figure 8.6. If you want, you can stretch the images in order to make it fit the entire screen.

Hint

Depending on the current size and dimension of the graphic file, the resulting quality and distortion of the image when stretched across the full application window may vary.

To stretch a graphic across the screen, you must determine the width and height of the screen. Once this information is acquired, you can use it to resize the rectangle within which the image is displayed.

To capture width and height information you can use the `GraphicsDevice` class's `Viewport` structure's `Width` and `Height` properties to retrieve the application window's width and height, as demonstrated here:

```
DisplayRect = new Rectangle(0, 0, GraphicsDevice.Viewport.Width,
    GraphicsDevice.Viewport.Height);
```

As you can see, this statement sets the coordinates for the rectangle, starting at coordinates 0, 0, with a width set equal to the width of the screen and a height set equal to the height of the screen. (See Figure 8.7.)

Hint

A *viewport* is a structure made up of four members—`X`, `Y`, `Width`, and `Height`. It defines the area within which a graphic is rendered. The `Viewport` structure belongs to the `GraphicsDevice` object, which itself is also an object that supports `Width` and `Height` properties of its own, representing the screen width and height.

To better understand how to fill the entire application window with a graphic, let's create a new XNA Windows application. This new application will be a modified version of the DisplayGraphics application. Begin by highlighting and copying all of the code statements that make up the DisplayGraphics application's Game1.cs file. Now, create a new XNA Windows application and name it Picture Viewer. Next, add Kittens.jpg to the application's content pipeline. Now paste the code statements you copied from the DisplayGraphics application into the Game1.cs file for your new application, replacing all existing statements. Next, change the application's namespace statement from

```
namespace DisplayGraphics
```

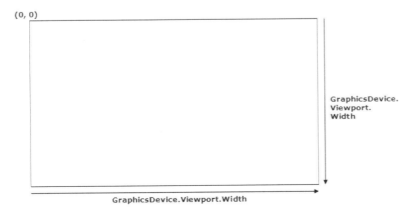

Figure 8.7
Retrieving screen width and height.

to

```
namespace Picture_Viewer
```

At this point, the Picture Viewer application operates identically to the DisplayGraphics application. Now it is time to change that, modifying the application so that it displays the picture in full screen. To make this happen, all you need to do is modify the application's Initialize() method. The changes to be made to the Initialize() method are shown below in bold.

```
protected override void Initialize()
{
    int PicWidth;   //Define variable used to specify picture width
    int PicHeight; //Define variable used to specify picture height

    //Set picture width and height to be the size of the window
    PicWidth = GraphicsDevice.Viewport.Width;
    PicHeight = GraphicsDevice.Viewport.Height;

    //Instantiate the rectangle
    DisplayRect = new Rectangle(0, 0, PicWidth, PicHeight);

    base.Initialize();
}
```

The first two statements in the Initialize() method define a pair of variables named PicWidth and PicHeight. The next two statements assign the width and height of the application window to the PicWidth and PicHeight variables. This data is retrieved using the Width and Height properties belonging to the GraphicsDevice class's Viewport structure. The last change you need to make to the Initialize() method is to modify the statement that instantiates the Rectangle object. As you can see, this statement has replaced width and height arguments of 640 and 480 with the PicWidth and PicHeight variables (e.g., the width and height of the application window).

Figure 8.8 shows how the Picture Viewer application looks when executed. Now the picture takes up the entire application window.

Creating an Electronic Picture Viewer

Other than displaying a window with an interesting background, there is not much to this application to keep the user interested. Let's make things more interesting by turning the Picture Viewer application into an electronic picture

Figure 8.8
Now the application uses the graphic to fill the entire window.

viewer that displays an assortment of different pictures at two-second intervals. To set this up, you need to make a number of changes to the Picture Viewer application.

For starters, you must add a couple of new picture files to the application. You'll find copies of two picture files named Newborns.jpg and Pup.jpg available for download from this book's companion web page located at www.courseptr.com/downloads. Once you have updated the application's content, you can start making the required code modifications.

The first set of changes to be made are to the application's game world data and as such are made at the beginning of the program, at the start of the Game1 class definition. These changes are shown below in bold.

```
public class Game1 : Microsoft.Xna.Framework.Game
{
    GraphicsDeviceManager graphics;
    SpriteBatch spriteBatch;

    int timer;               //Used to control timer execution

    //Define texture variables used to display graphics
```

```
Texture2D Kittens;
Texture2D Pup;
Texture2D Newborns;
Texture2D SelectedPic;

//Define rectangle with which to display graphics
Rectangle DisplayRect;
   .
   .
   .
```

As you can see, a number of new code statements have been added. The first of these statements define an integer variable named timer, which the application will use later as part of an internal timer mechanism that controls the display of pictures at two-second intervals. The rest of the code statements define a series of variables. These first two variables (Pup and Newborns) will be used to reference the additional two graphic files. The third variable (SelectedPic) will be used to specify which of the application's graphics should be displayed at any given moment in time.

The next set of code changes need to be made to the Initialize() method. These changes are highlighted below in bold.

```
protected override void Initialize()
{
    int PicWidth;   //Define variable used to specify picture width
    int PicHeight; //Define variable used to specify picture height

    timer = 0;        //Set timer to zero
    SelectedPic = Kittens;  //Specify the default picture

    //Set picture width and height to be the size of the window
    PicWidth = GraphicsDevice.Viewport.Width;
    PicHeight = GraphicsDevice.Viewport.Height;

    //Instantiate the rectangle
    DisplayRect = new Rectangle(0, 0, PicWidth, PicHeight);

    base.Initialize();
}
```

The first highlighted statement assigned a starting value of 0 to the timer variable. The second highlighted statement sets the value of SelectedPic to the value assigned to `Kittens`, specifying the image that is initially displayed by the application.

Now that you have defined the variables the application will use to reference the application's graphic files, you need to modify the `LoadContent()` method so that it loads the two additional graphic files into memory. The code statement changes that make this happen are highlighted below in bold.

```
protected override void LoadContent()
{
    //Create a new SpriteBatch, which can be used to draw textures.
    spriteBatch = new SpriteBatch(GraphicsDevice);

    //Load the application's graphic files
    Kittens = Content.Load<Texture2D>(@"Kittens");
    Pup = Content.Load<Texture2D>(@"Pup");
    Newborns = Content.Load<Texture2D>(@"Newborns");
}
```

In order to control the timing of the application so that it displays a different picture every two seconds, you need to implement a timer mechanism, making use of the `timer` variable, which you just added to the application's game data. To do so, modify the `Update()` method as shown here.

```
protected override void Update(GameTime gameTime)
{
    // Allows the game to exit
    if (GamePad.GetState(PlayerIndex.One).Buttons.Back ==
        ButtonState.Pressed)
        this.Exit();

    //Switch picture every two seconds
    switch (timer)
    {
        case 0:
            SelectedPic = Kittens;
            break;
        case 120:
            SelectedPic = Pup;
            break;
        case 240:
            SelectedPic = Newborns;
            break;
```

```
        case 360:
            timer = -1;
            break;
    }
    timer++; //Increment value by one

    base.Update(gameTime);
}
```

As you can see, these statements test the value assigned to the timer variable (defined at the beginning of the program and assigned an initial value of 0). Using a switch code block, four case statements are specified that change the value assigned to SelectedPic when the value of time is equal to 0, 120, 240, and 360, respectively. The value assigned to SelectedPic determines which image file is displayed on the screen.

Remember that by default the Update() method executes 60 times a second. So timer will be equal to 0 when the application first starts. As a result, the value of SelectedPic is set to Kittens. At 2 seconds (e.g., when timer = 120) SelectedPic is set to Pup. At 4 seconds, the value of SelectedPic is set to Newborns. In addition, the value of timer is reset back to zero, restarting the sequence again. Also note that the value of time is automatically incremented by 1 at the end of the Update() method.

The last change you need to make is highlighted below in the Draw() method.

```
protected override void Draw(GameTime gameTime)
{
    GraphicsDevice.Clear(Color.CornflowerBlue);

    //Draw the currently specified picture on the application window
    spriteBatch.Begin();
    spriteBatch.Draw(SelectedPic, DisplayRect, Color.White);
    spriteBatch.End();

    base.Draw(gameTime);
}
```

Instead of hardcoding the variable name of the picture to be displayed (e.g., Kitten, Pup, or Newborns), the selectedPic variable is used within the sprite-Batch.Draw() statement. This way the application displays whichever picture the value of selectedPic has been set to.

Figure 8.9
The Electronic Picture Viewer application displays a different picture every two seconds.

Once you have made all of the changes that have been outlined, you are ready to test your new electronic picture viewer. Figure 8.9 shows a series of three screen shots, showing each of the three pictures displayed by the application as it executes.

Summary

In this chapter you learned how to make your XNA games much more interesting through the use of graphics. You learned about the various types of graphic types that XNA supports and how XNA's content pipeline manages the graphics you import into your applications. In addition to learning how to add and display graphics, you learned how to control the placement and size of graphics in the game window. Using the information provided in this chapter, you learned how to create an electronic picture viewer application and in doing so established a foundation needed in Chapters 10 and 11 to begin creating arcade-style computer games.

CHAPTER 9

ADDING SOUND EFFECTS
AND BACKGROUND MUSIC

Up to this point in the book, all of the sample applications have had one thing in common: they have been mute. Quality sound effects and background music are essential components of computer games. They help set the mood and to make things more exciting. Effective use of sound effects can also provide an additional means of communicating with game players, letting them know when certain types of events occur.

An overview of the major topics covered in this chapter includes learning:

- About the different types of audio files supported by XNA

- How to add audio files to your XNA applications

- How to play and pause audio playback

- How to loop audio playback and to control volume, pitch, and pan

Adding Audio to Your Games

Just about every computer game makes use of sound effects and background music. Sound effects are played at critical moments to help provide added emphasis to key events, such as when two objects collide or a player scores a point. Background music, on the other hand, is typically used to provide additional atmosphere to games, helping to establish a mood that draws players further into the game.

Prior to XNA Game Studio 3.0, XNA game developers had to use a tool called the Microsoft *Cross-Platform Audio Creation Tool* or *XACT* in order to add and manage sound playback in XNA games. XACT is a powerful tool, providing the ability to edit sound volume and pitch as well as do things like create custom sound tracks. XACT, shown in Figure 9.1, is a sort of pint-sized sound studio system. It takes a bit of learning to get used to and arguably is a bit of overkill for many XNA games. XACT's biggest problem is that it only supports game development on the PC and Xbox 360; it does not support the Zune player.

With the advent of XNA Game Studio 3.0, Microsoft simplified the integration of audio in XNA applications through the introduction of a new streamlined audio *API* (*application programming interface*) that works with the PC, Xbox 360, and the Zune Player. The new API does not have all the advanced bells and whistles as XACT, but is powerful enough to get the job done and is much easier to learn.

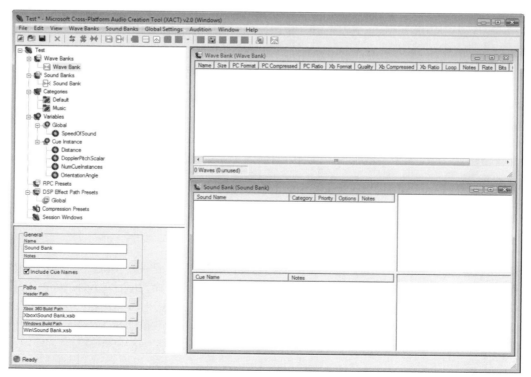

Figure 9.1
XACT is an advanced audio development tool.

Hint

We'll use the new XNA API exclusively in this book. If you wish to learn more about XACT, consult with XNA's Help files.

Adding Audio Files to Your XNA Applications

The new audio API supports the playback of .wav, .wma, and .mp3 audio files. With the API, you work with audio files just like any other resource. The first step is to add the audio file to your application by right-clicking on the Content folder located in the Solution Explorer window, selecting Add > Existing Item, locating your audio file, and then clicking on Add. This loads the audio file into the content pipeline, enabling you to programmatically refer to and manage its playback.

Defining and Locating Sound Resources

The next step, once you have put an audio file into the content pipeline, is to define a variable that you can use to set up a reference to it, as demonstrated here:

```
SoundEffect MySound;
```

As you can see, you must specify a type of SoundEffect when defining the variable. At this point, you are ready to load the audio file by using the Load method, as demonstrated here.

```
MySound = Content.Load<SoundEffect>(@"Surprise");
```

Here, Surprise is the filename (less its file extension) of an audio file that has previously been added to the application.

Controlling Sound Playback

Once loaded, you can play the audio file. To do so, you must execute the SoundEffect class's Play method. When executed, this method will return an object of type SoundEffectInstance, to which you can assign a variable that can then be used to control audio playback, executing actions like play and pause. You can also change playback volume. For example, the following statement could be used to initiate playback of the previously defined and loaded audio file.

```
SoundEffectInstance MyNewSound = MySound.play();
```

Hint

If the audio file's contents are suitable for a game's background music, you could place this statement inside the application's `LoadContent` method just after the preceding `Load` statements in order to start its playback. Similarly, if the audio file contains a sound suitable for use as a special sound effect, such as an explosion or a gun shot, you could strategically execute its playback from a well placed location in the source code controlled by the `Update` method.

Once the previous statement has been executed, you can use the `SoundEffect-Instance` object to manage audio playback, as demonstrated here:

```
MyNewSound.Pause();
```

Similarly, you can resume playback again by executing the following statement.

```
MyNewSound.Play();
```

Supported Audio File Formats

XNA works with three types of sound files, each of which is outlined in Table 9.1.

XNA supports the use of wave files for sound effects. A *wave* file is a compressed audio file used in games to play a sound effect. MP3 files usually have a higher quality playback than WMA, offering CD-quality sound. As a result, MP3 files have become the defacto standard for digital music files. You can create .wma and .wav sound files using the Windows Sound recorder application supplied with Microsoft Windows. You can also use any number of third-party audio applications to create .mp3, .wma, and .wav files. You'll find plenty of freeware and shareware audio applications ready for download on the internet.

Table 9.1 XNA Supported Audio File Types

File Type	Description
.wav	Compressed audio files that store short sounds used to play sound effects in games and applications.
.mp3	Moving Picture Experts Group (MPEG-1 Audio Layer 3) files are used to store digital music. In order to play .mp3 files, XNA must first decompress it. This extra step takes time, making .mp3 files inappropriate for sound effects. However, .mp3 files are commonly used to add background music playback in games.
.wma	Windows Media Audio files are a compressed audio file type created by Microsoft for use with Windows Media Player.

Trap

You will also find plenty of audio files on the internet. Make sure that you carefully follow any copyright restrictions for any audio files you download.

Adding Sound Effects to Projects

The clever use of sound effects can significantly enhance the quality of computer games. To demonstrate how easy it is to add a sound effect to your XNA applications, let's work on a quick example. Begin by creating a new project named SoundTest. Next, right-click on Content in the Solution Explorer window and click on Add > Existing Item, as shown in Figure 9.2. Locate and select a wave file and then click on Add.

An icon representing the audio file will be listed as an available resource in the Content section of the Solution Explorer window, as shown in Figure 9.3.

You can verify the resource name that XNA has assigned to the audio file by selecting it in Solution Explorer and then viewing its property settings. If the Properties window is not visible, you can display it by clicking on View > Properties Window.

Figure 9.2
Adding an audio file to your XNA project.

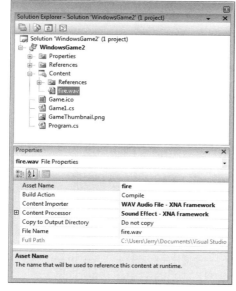

Figure 9.3
A wave file named fire.wav has been added to the XNA project.

Hint

> Wave files are best used for sound effects because they are small and load quickly. If you do not have your own wave files that you can use, you'll find one named fire.wav on this book's companion web page located at www.courseptr.com/downloads/.

Once added, XNA's Content Manager makes the audio file available to your game, allowing it to programmatically control its playback. Next, place a statement defining a SoundEffect variable at the beginning of the Game1 class, as shown here.

```
public class Game1 : Microsoft.Xna.Framework.Game
{
    GraphicsDeviceManager graphics;
    SpriteBatch spriteBatch;

    //Define a variable of type SoundEffect to be used to reference and
    //control an audio file
    SoundEffect fire;
}
```

Once defined, you need to associate the audio file with the variable. To do so, execute the load method within the LoadContent() method as demonstrated here. Using the LoadContent() method to handle this operation ensures that the special effect will be loaded into memory and made available when needed once the application starts running.

```
protected override void LoadContent()
{
    // Create a new SpriteBatch, which can be used to draw textures.
    spriteBatch = new SpriteBatch(GraphicsDevice);

    //Associate and load the audio file with the fire variable
    fire = Content.Load<SoundEffect>("fire");
}
```

As you can see, there is no difference between how the load method is used here and how it was used in Chapter 8 to load a graphic file, except that a type of SoundEffect is specified in place of Texture2D.

Hint

The SoundEffect class's play method is intended to play small wave files. Since wave files are loaded into memory when your applications run, they can be played quickly when needed to support special sound effects in your games. Since wave files are typically small files containing small audio sounds, they do not take up a lot of memory.

Now that you have defined a SoundEffect variable and used it to load the wave file, you can play it using the SoundEffect class's Play() method. To make things simple, let's use a gamepad control to initiate playback of the special effect. To do so, go back and modify the game world data located at the beginning of the Game1 class, as shown here:

```
public class Game1 : Microsoft.Xna.Framework.Game
{
    GraphicsDeviceManager graphics;
    SpriteBatch spriteBatch;

    //Define a variable of type SoundEffect to be used to reference and
    //control an audio file
    SoundEffect fire;

    GamePadState GamePadOneState;  //Store current gamepad state
    GamePadState GamePadOnePrevState;  //Store previous gamepad state
}
```

These two new variables will be used to store current and previous GamePad state, allowing the application to determine when one of the gamepad's button controls has been pushed for the first time. Next, modify the Update() method as shown below in order to collect GamePad state, initiating playback of the special effect when the A button on the gamepad is pressed.

```
protected override void Update(GameTime gameTime)
{
    //Capture current gamepad state
    GamePadOneState = GamePad.GetState(PlayerIndex.One);

    // Allows the game to exit
    if (GamePad.GetState(PlayerIndex.One).Buttons.Back ==
        ButtonState.Pressed) this.Exit();

    //Determine if the gamepad button has just been pressed
    if (GamePadOnePrevState.Buttons.A == ButtonState.Released)
    {
        if (GamePadOneState.Buttons.A == ButtonState.Pressed)
        {
            fire.Play();
        }
    }

    //Save the current gamepad state
    GamePadOnePrevState = GamePadOneState;

    base.Update(gameTime);
}
```

Okay, go ahead and run your XNA application and let's see what happens. If all goes well, you will see a window appear with a light blue background. Make sure you have a gamepad attached to your computer's USB port. Now press the gamepad's A button and you should hear the sound effect play.

Hint

Most game sound effects are triggered to play when specific events occur during game play and not when the player does something with a game control. For example, most games play sound effects when objects come into contact with one another. You will see an example of this in Chapter 10, where you will learn how to create your first real XNA game.

Exercising Additional Control of Audio Playback

By default the Play method plays an audio file one time and then halts. It does so at the computer's current volume level. However, with a little tweaking, the Play method can be made to:

- Loop audio playback

- Adjust playback volume

- Change pitch

- Change pan settings

In order to use the `Play` method to perform any of the actions outlined above, you must use the following syntax.

```
InstanceName = VariableName.Play(Volume, Pitch, Pan, Boolean);
```

Here, *InstanceName* is the name you are assigning to the `SoundEffectInstance` object that is being generated. *VariableName* is the name of a variable previously assigned to an audio file. `Volume` is a numeric value between 0 and 1 specifying playback volume level (0 equals no volume and 1 equals maximum volume). `Pitch` is a numeric value between −1 and 1, specifying the pitch at which playback occurs. `Pan` is a numeric value between −1 and 1 (left and right). `Boolean` is a boolean value of `true` or `false` (a value of `true` instructs the statements to play back the audio file in a loop). So, for example, say you wanted to play an audio in a loop at half value. You could do so, as demonstrated here:

```
MyAudioInstance = MyAudioFile.Play(.5, 0, 0, true);
```

Setting the Mood with Background Music

As has already been stated, a key component in most video games is the background music that is continuously played during game play. *Pac-Man* is a classic example. Sure, various special effect sounds occur as the Pac-Man runs the maze chewing up little yellow dots or as he gobbles down the ghosts once they have turned blue. But just as important is the Pac-Man theme music that is forever playing in the background.

Wave files are used for special effects because they are small and can be easily loaded into memory, where they can be quickly played on demand. However, they are usually not well suited for use as background music, which is where .mp3 and .wma files come into play. Audio music files tend to be larger and take longer to play. In addition, most games repeatedly play (loop the playback of) background music, ensuring that it runs from the moment the game starts until it ends.

Working with the Computer's Media Player

If you have wave files that contain music, you can use the `SoundEffect` object's `play` method's looping capability to add background music to your XNA games. Doing so places a copy of the audio file into memory, which is okay if the wave file is not too large. However, if the audio file you are working with is a large one, this is not an efficient use of system resources. Instead, it is better to make use of .mp3 and .wma files and to play them using the `MediaPlayer` class.

Hint

The `SoundEffect` class's `play` method is intended to play small wave files. Since wave files are loaded into memory when your applications run, they can be played quickly when needed to support special sound effects in your games. Since wave files are typically small files containing small audio sounds, they do not take up a lot of memory.

The `MediaPlayer` class allows you to play, pause, resume, and stop playback of .mp3 and .wma audio files (as background music). The `MediaPlayer` class also has methods that allow you to repeat audio playback and to control volume level.

Hint

The `MediaPlayer` class is an example of a static class. A *static* class is a class that is readily available to your program and does not need to be instantiated using the `new` keyword in order to access its methods and properties.

Loading a .wma or .mp3 File

.mp3 and .wma audio files are usually large files. As such, they are most efficiently managed via the `MediaPlayer` class. The `MediaPlayer` class conveniently provides its own `play` method that you can use to playback an .mp3 or .wma audio file. To work with it, you must first load your .mp3 or .wma file into your application by right-clicking on the Content folder located in the Solution Explorer window, clicking on Add > Existing Item, and then locating and selecting an audio file and clicking on the Add button.

Associating Variables with Your Audio Files

Once you have imported an .mp3 or .wma audio file into your application, you need to define a variable as part of your application's game world data, as demonstrated here:

```
Song MyMusicFile;
```

As you can see, an object type of `song` must be specified.

Loading Audio Files

Once you have defined a variable for your audio file, you must load it, as demonstrated here:

```
MyMusicFile = Content.Load<Song>(@"resource");
```

Here, *resource* is the name that XNA assigns to the audio file when you load it into the content pipeline.

Playing Background Music

At this point you are ready to initiate the playback of the audio file. To do so, you must use the MediaPlayer class's Play method.

```
MediaPlayer.Play(MusicFile);
```

Here, *MusicFile* represents the name that XNA assigned to the audio file when you added it to the content pipeline. The MediaPlayer class supports a number of other methods that affect playback. These methods include:

- **Pause.** Pauses the currently playing song.

- **Resume.** Resumes song playback from the point at which it was paused.

- **Stop.** Halts song playback.

The MediaPlayer class also has a number of properties that you can use to set or retrieve media player state. These properties include:

- **Volume.** Sets and retrieves media player volume (0.0f (silent) to 1.0f (full volume))

- **IsMuted.** Sets and retrieves media player mute status (a value assignment of true enables mute)

- **IsRepeating.** Sets and retrieves media player repeat state (a value assignment of true enables repeat)

Creating the Music Machine Application

To further your understanding of how to play .mp3 and .wma files using the MediaPlayer class, let's create a new application called the Music Machine. Figure 9.4 shows how the Music Machine application will look when initially started. As you

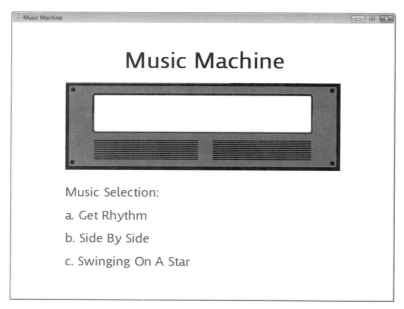

Figure 9.4
A look at the Music Machine application when it is first started.

can see, the application displays a graphic image of a media player device along with a list of songs that can be played.

The game is controlled using a keyboard. So to play the first song you would press the A key. The B and C keys can be pressed to play the other songs. In addition, you can press the Space key at any time to halt sound playback. Figure 9.5 shows how the game loops when playing a song.

Importing the Audio Files

To create a copy of this application yourself, you will need access to three .mp3 or .wma files. Once you have selected the audio files you want to use, add them to your new XNA project by right-clicking on the Content folder located in the Solution Explorer window, clicking on Add > Existing Item, and then locating and selecting an audio file and clicking on the Add button.

Importing the Graphic Files

As you can see in Figures 9.4 and 9.5, the Music Machine displays both a graphic image as well as text at various font sizes. Once you have added three of your own music files to the content pipeline, you'll need to add the graphic representing the

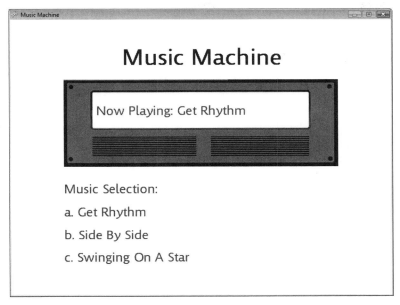

Figure 9.5
The Music Machine displays the names of the songs when playing them.

media player to the application. You will find a copy of this graphic available on this book's companion website located at www.courseptr.com/downloads/.

Importing and Configuring Fonts

The last of piece of content that you need to add to the application are the two fonts that are used to display text on the application window. Begin by right-clicking on Content and then click on Add > New Item. The Add new Item – Content window will appear. Select the Sprite Font icon and click on Add. XNA adds SpriteFont1.spritefont to the project. The contents of the new Sprite Font file are displayed in the code editor in the form of an XML file. Locate and modify the ⟨Size⟩ tag entry as shown here:

```
<!--
Size is a float value, measured in points. Modify this value to change
the size of the font.
-->
<Size>20</Size>
```

This will set the size of the font to 20 points. You will use this font when displaying the names of the songs that you added to the application. Close the

`SpriteFont1.spritefont` file. Now repeat the above steps again to add a second font to the application and then locate and configure its `<Size>`, as shown here:

```
<!--
Size is a float value, measured in points. Modify this value to change
the size of the font.
-->
<Size>36</Size>
```

This font will be used to display the name of the application at the top of the application window. As such, it will need to be displayed in a relatively large, bold font. To make the font display in bold, locate and configure its `<Style>` as shown here.

```
<!--
Style controls the style of the font. Valid entries are "Regular", "Bold",
"Italic", and "Bold, Italic", and are case sensitive.
-->
<Style>Bold</Style>
```

At this point, your application should have all of the resources shown in Figure 9.6.

Trick

You can rename any of the filenames shown in the Solution Explorer window to make them more descriptive. To do so, right-click on filename, click on Rename, as shown in Figure 9.7, and then type in a new name for the file.

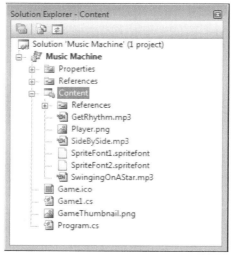

Figure 9.6
The Music Machine application makes use of multiple types of content.

Figure 9.7
Renaming a resource after it has been added to your XNA application.

You may want to double-check on the names that XNA has assigned to your content resources, just to make sure that there are no surprises. To do so, select each resource one at a time and then look at the Asset Name field in the Properties window, as shown in Figure 9.8.

Time to Start Coding

The first step in generating the program code for the Music Machine application is to define variables that will be used to work with the application's audio files, fonts, and graphic file. In addition, you will need to define a `Rectangle` variable for use in displaying the graphic as well as a `string` variable, which will be used to store and display the name of the currently playing song when the application is running. The statements that accomplish all this are shown next and are part of the game world data; as such, you must place them at the beginning of the `Game1` class, outside of any of the program's methods.

```
public class Game1 : Microsoft.Xna.Framework.Game
{
    GraphicsDeviceManager graphics;
    SpriteBatch spriteBatch;

    //Define variables of type Song to be used to reference and
    //control mp3 file playback
    Song MusicFile1;
```

Figure 9.8
When in doubt you can verify the name assigned to a resource by viewing its Properties window.

```
        Song MusicFile2;
        Song MusicFile3;

        //Define variables of type Font to be used to display text
        SpriteFont font;
        SpriteFont boldFont;

        //Define variable of type Texture2D for use in displaying a graphic
        Texture2D player;

        //Define variable of type Rectangle to be used when displaying
        //graphic
        Rectangle DisplayRect;

        //Define variable of type String to be used to store text message
        String msg = "";

            .
            .
            .
```

In order to display the graphic media player image, you will need to instantiate a Rectangle object and position it in the upper part of the application window. To do so, modify the Initialize() method as shown here:

```
protected override void Initialize()
{
    //Instantiate and define coordinates for a rectangle object
    DisplayRect = new Rectangle(112, 130, 576, 189);

    base.Initialize();
}
```

Now it is time to load all of the fonts, audio files, and the application's graphic file. To do so, modify the LoadContent() method as shown here:

```
protected override void LoadContent()
{
    // Create a new SpriteBatch, which can be used to draw textures.
    spriteBatch = new SpriteBatch(GraphicsDevice);

    //Load the application's fonts
    font = Content.Load<SpriteFont>("SpriteFont1");
    boldFont = Content.Load<SpriteFont>("SpriteFont2");

    //Load the application's song files
    MusicFile1 = Content.Load<Song>(@"GetRhythm");
    MusicFile2 = Content.Load<Song>(@"SideBySide");
    MusicFile3 = Content.Load<Song>(@"SwingingOnAStar");

    //Load the application's graphic file
    player = Content.Load<Texture2D>(@"Player");
}
```

If you elected to rename any of the resource files in your application, you will need to change the statements above to reflect the asset names. Also, you will need to modify the three statements that load the audio files, substituting the asset names assigned to audio files that you chose to include in your copy of the Music Machine application.

The Music Machine application is designed to be controlled via a keyboard. It will play a different song depending on whether the A, B, or C key is pressed. It will halt song playback when the Space key is pressed. In addition, the application will terminate its execution when the Escape key is pressed. The code statements

that make all this happen must be placed within the Update() method, as shown
here:

```
protected override void Update(GameTime gameTime)
{

    KeyboardState keys = Keyboard.GetState();

    // Allows the game to exit
    if (keys.IsKeyDown(Keys.Escape))
        this.Exit();

    //Play the selected song when the A, B or C key is pressed and
    //display a message showing the selected song
    if (keys.IsKeyDown(Keys.A))
    {
        MediaPlayer.Play(MusicFile1);
        msg = "Now Playing: Get Rhythm";
    }
    if (keys.IsKeyDown(Keys.B))
    {
        MediaPlayer.Play(MusicFile2);
        msg = "Now Playing: Side By Side";
    }
    if (keys.IsKeyDown(Keys.C))
    {
        MediaPlayer.Play(MusicFile3);
        msg = "Now Playing: Swinging On A Star";
    }

    //Allow the user to halt song playback by pressing the Space key
    if (keys.IsKeyDown(Keys.Space))
    {
        MediaPlayer.Pause();
        msg = "";
    }

    base.Update(gameTime);
}
```

Note that whenever the user selects a song, a text string containing the name of
the song is assigned to the msg variable. You will need to modify these three
statements that set song names to reflect the name of the audio files that you

added to your version of the Music Machine application. Also note that an empty string ("") is assigned to msg when the Space key is pressed. The contents of the msg variable will be drawn on top of the media player graphic when the application runs in order to identify the name of the song being played.

At this point all that remains is to add the programming logic that lays out the coordinates where things are drawn on the application window in order to create the application's user interface. This is done using a series of Vector objects, along with the execution of a series of SpriteBatch class DrawString and Draw method statements. The code statements that do all this go inside the Draw() method as shown here:

```
protected override void Draw(GameTime gameTime)
{
    //Clear the screen and redraw its background color as white
    GraphicsDevice.Clear(Color.White);

    //Set the coordinates at which the application title is displayed
    Vector2 textVector1 = new Vector2(235, 50);

    //Set the coordinates at which the application message is displayed
    Vector2 textVector2 = new Vector2(180, 180);

    //Set the coordinates at which the Music Selection menu is displayed
    Vector2 textVector3 = new Vector2(112, 350);

    //Set the coordinates at which the music menu is displayed
    Vector2 textVector4 = new Vector2(112, 400);
    Vector2 textVector5 = new Vector2(112, 450);
    Vector2 textVector6 = new Vector2(112, 500);

    //Display the application's title, graphic and menu
    spriteBatch.Begin();
    spriteBatch.DrawString(boldFont, "Music Machine", textVector1,
        Color.Black);
    spriteBatch.Draw(player, DisplayRect, Color.White);
    spriteBatch.DrawString(font, msg, textVector2, Color.Purple);
    spriteBatch.DrawString(font, "Music Selection:", textVector3,
        Color.Blue);
    spriteBatch.DrawString(font, "a. Get Rhythm", textVector4, Color.Blue);
    spriteBatch.DrawString(font, "b. Side By Side", textVector5,
        Color.Blue);
```

```
spriteBatch.DrawString(font, "c. Swinging On A Star", textVector6,
    Color.Blue);

spriteBatch.End();

base.Draw(gameTime);
}
```

That's it. Assuming that you have followed along carefully and have not skipped any steps or made any typos, your copy of the Music Machine application should be good to go.

Hint

If you do not have time to re-create this application, you will find a working copy of it ready for download on the book's companion website located at www.courseptr.com/downloads. Note however that this copy of the application does not include any music files. You will still need to supply three .mp3 or .wma files and make the appropriate name changes within the program code as previously identified.

Summary

In this chapter you learned the ins and outs of XNA's support for audio file playback. Quality sound effects and background music are essential elements of computer games. They help establish a mood and to make things exciting. Audio playback is an effective communication tool, providing you with the ability to inform the player about all kinds of events using sounds like explosions, gun shots, and so on. Using the information and examples provided, you now have the ability to significantly enhance your XNA games and applications through the application of background music and special audio effects.

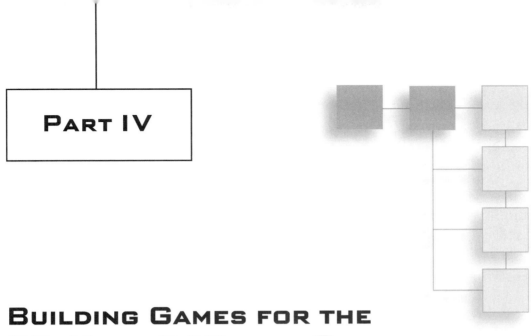

PART IV

BUILDING GAMES FOR THE PC, XBOX 360, AND ZUNE

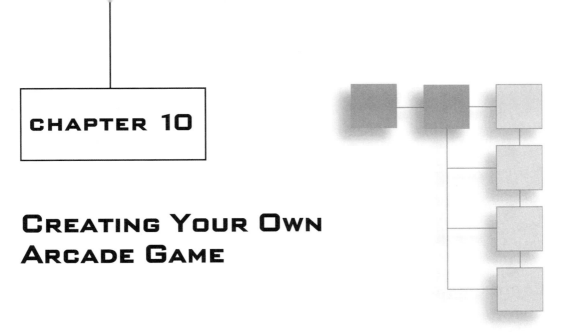

CHAPTER 10

CREATING YOUR OWN ARCADE GAME

At this point in the book, you have learned a lot about how to program with C#. You have also learned many of the basic steps involved in developing XNA applications. This chapter will teach you a few more fundamental game development techniques and then will help you tie everything together by guiding you through the development of your first real computer game, XNA Breakout.

The major topics covered in this chapter include learning how to:

- Add a splash screen to your application
- Create and manage different game states
- Properly size game sprites and maintain their proper appearance
- Move sprites around the screen
- Detect collisions between sprites

Key Features Found in Most Computer Games

Okay, so by now you know how to display text, draw, and position graphics on the screen as well as how to integrate sound effects into your XNA applications. To create your own computer games, you need to learn how to do a few more things, including learning how to:

- Manage game state

- Properly manage the size and shape of sprites

- Move sprites around

- Detect when sprites move off the screen

- Detect when sprites collide

In addition to the game features listed above, you also need to know how to run your games in full screen mode and how to deal with display overscan, as discussed later in this chapter.

Controlling a Game's State

Typically, most games have different states. They often start by displaying a welcome screen with instructions or menu options. The game may switch states when the player clicks on a button control or clicks on a menu item. Games may also support a paused state, allowing the player to temporarily halt and then later resume play. These are just a few of the many states games may support.

You can use a variable to support the transition between different states. For example, you could add a variable named stateOfGame to the application's game world data, as shown here:

```
bool stateOfGame = false;
```

Here, a variable of type Boolean has been defined and assigned an initial value of false. Using this variable, you can support a game with two states, where a value of false indicates one state and a value of true indicates another state. Alternatively, you could use a string variable instead and assign different values to it, each of which would represent a different game state.

Using the Boolean variable previously defined in an XNA game, you could control games with two states, a play state and a startup state. You would need to refer to the value of this variable in both the Upgrade() and Draw() methods to determine game state in order to know what statements to process. In addition, you will need to modify the variable's value during game execution in order to toggle it to the appropriate state. For example, you might modify the application's Update() method as shown in bold:

```
protected override void Update(GameTime gameTime)
{
    // Allows the game to exit
```

```
if (GamePad.GetState(PlayerIndex.One).Buttons.Back ==
  ButtonState.Pressed)
{
    this.Exit();
}

//Retrieve gamepad state data
GamePadState gamePad1 = GamePad.GetState(PlayerIndex.One);

if (stateOfGame == true)  //A value of true indicates active game play
{
    //Place statements that control game play here
}
else
{
    //Place statements that display start-up screen here
}

base.Update(gameTime);
```

}Alternatively, you might use a `switch` code block to determine which statements should be executed based on game states, as shown in bold:

```
protected override void Draw(GameTime gameTime)
{
    GraphicsDevice.Clear(Color.CornflowerBlue);
    Vector2 textVector1 = new Vector2(40, 30);

    spriteBatch.Begin();
    switch (stateOfGame)
    {
        case false:
            //Add statements here that draw the game's sprites
            break;
        case true:
            //Add statements here that displays the splash screen
            break;
    }
    spriteBatch.End();

    base.Draw(gameTime);
}
```

Here, the statements that are executed in the Draw() method depend on what state the game is in. As such, keeping track of game state and assigning a value to the stateOfGame variable is very important. So, if your game is designed to start by displaying a menu or splash screen, you will want to set the variable to false at the beginning of the game and then change its value to true when the player signals that he is ready to play, as demonstrated here:

```
//Start game play when the player presses the gamepad's A button
if (gamePad1.Buttons.A == ButtonState.Pressed)
{
    stateOfgame = true;
}
```

These statements, which would be placed at the beginning of the Update() method, set the value of stateOfGame to true when the player presses the gamepad's A button. Once the variable's value is changed, the program statements that manage game play in the Update() and Draw() methods will start executing. At some point, game play will end. This might occur if, for example, the player runs out of lives. If this were the case, a statement like the following could be executed, in order to change game state back to false.

```
if (playerLives == 0)
{
    stateOfGame = false;
}
```

Once game state is changed as shown above, the statements that display the game's splash screen would be executed.

Setting Sprite Size and Shape

As has been previously stated, the graphics that you add, move around, and interact with in your XNA games are referred to as sprites. Sprites are generated by defining a Texture2D variable and then loading graphic content. Sprite location on the screen is determined by the Rectangle objects in which they are managed. Placement of the sprites is managed by program code managed from the Update() method and made visible on the screen via statements managed by the Draw() method.

When developing games to be run on Windows computers, you can run your applications in a standard window or in full-screen mode (as demonstrated later in this chapter). When developing games to be run on the Xbox, there are other considerations, such as the size, type, and resolution of the television the player will be using—which you can't know in advance. And if you are planning on generating games for the Zune player, you have to take the limited size of the screen into consideration.

Given all the possible screen sizes and resolutions, it's essential that you design your games so they resize dynamically to match the screen on which they are being played. The first step in doing so is to determine the width and height of the screen as your game initializes. Do this by defining a pair of variables as part of your game world data, as shown here:

```
float windowWidth;
float windowHeight;
```

These variables have been defined as floating point in order to allow for greater precision. Once the variables have been defined, you can use the Viewport object's Width and Height properties to store the screen dimensions as shown here in bold.

```
protected override void Initialize()
{
    windowWidth = graphics.GraphicsDevice.Viewport.Width;
    windowHeight = graphics.GraphicsDevice.Viewport.Height;

    base.Initialize();
}
```

Once you know the width and height of the screen on which your game is executing, you can adjust the size of its sprites. When doing so you must be careful not to distort the appearance of the sprites by allowing their width and height *ratios* to be changed. You can determine the correct width to height *aspect ratio* of a sprite by dividing its width by its height. Every text has width and height properties, which you can use to retrieve this data, as demonstrated here:

```
float graphicRatio = (float) ballTexture.Width / ballTexture.Height;
```

Now that you have determined the width/height ratio of the sprite, you can use it to adjust the size of the sprite in order to ensure it is appropriate for the screen resolution the game is being played on. To do so, you must add another variable to game world data, as shown here:

```
float ballSize = 0.04f;
```

The purpose of this variable is to specify the scale at which the sprite should be drawn. In this case, a floating-point value of 0.04f will be used to adjust sprite size to 1/25 the size of the screen (0.05 equals a twentieth and 0.1 represents a tenth, etc), as demonstrated here:

```
ballRect.Width = (int)((windowWidth * ballSize) + 0.5f);
float graphicRatio = (float)ballTexture.Width / ballTexture.Height;
ballRect.Height = (int)((ballRect.Width / graphicRatio) + 0.5f);
```

The first statement sets the width at which the sprite will be displayed by multiplying the width of the screen times the value of ballSize (0.04f). A value of 0.05f is then added and the final floating-point value is then converted to an integer. The reason that the additional 0.0f value is added to the formula is to ensure that rounding occurs properly when working with floating-point data. Floating-point data always rounds down so a value of 10.99999 would round down to 10. By adding 0.05f to 10.99999, you ensure that it rounds down to 11, which is more accurate. Likewise, adding 0.05f to a value of 10.49999 would result in a rounded value of 10.

The second statement sets the sprite's width and height ratio, thus ensuring that it does not get distorted. The last statement sets the sprite's height by dividing its width by its calculated ratio.

Hint

Note the use of (int) and (float) in the preceding statements. They allow for the explicit conversion of a value from one type to another. In this example, floating-point numbers are used to ensure the greatest possible accuracy, but things must be converted back to integer values before they are applied.

Moving Things Around

Most games depend on the movement and interaction of sprites on the screen. For example, in a game like *Pong*, three sprites are used to represent the paddles and a ball. The ball must bounce around the screen while at the same time the players must be able to move their paddles in order to intercept and deflect the ball back to their opponent's side of the screen.

In order to manage a sprite movement on the screen, you need to define four sets of variables, as demonstrated here:

```
float ballX;
float ballY;
float ballXSpeed;
```

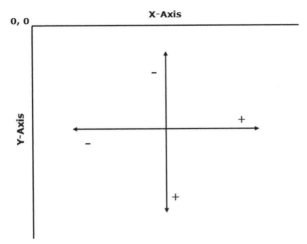

Figure 10.1
Sprite movement is managed by increasing or decreasing the sprite's X and Y coordinate assignments.

```
float ballYSpeed;
```

The first two variables will be used to store the sprite's current coordinate location. The second two variables will be used to store the current speed and direction of the sprite. Sprite movement is depicted in Figure 10.1.

The `ballXSpeed` and `ballYSpeed` variables are used to control the speed and direction that the sprite will move and can be set in the `Initialize()` method, as shown next. It is important that their values be calculated based on the current screen dimensions. This way the sprite will move across the screen at an appropriate speed regardless of its size.

```
protected override void Initialize()
{
    ballXSpeed = windowWidth / 140.0f;
    ballYSpeed = ballXSpeed;
    base.Initialize();
}
```

Note that in the first statement the value of `ballXSpeed` is set to `windowWidth` divided by `140.0f`. In this instance, `140.0f` represents the number of ticks of the clock that it will take for the sprite to move across the screen. Remember, the `Update()` method executes 60 ticks per second. The second statement sets the value of `ballYSpeed` equal to `ballXSpeed`. As a result, the ball will move at the same speed across both axes.

A sprite is moved to the right by adding a positive value to its X coordinate. A sprite is moved down by adding a positive value to its Y coordinate. Likewise, a sprite is moved up and to the left by adding negative values to its X and Y coordinates. To control sprite movement, you would add statements like those shown here to the program's Update() method.

```
ballX = ballX + ballXSpeed;
ballY = ballY + ballYSpeed;
ballRect.X = (int)(ballX + 0.5f);
ballRect.Y = (int)(ballY + 0.5f);
```

The first statement updates the sprite's location on the X axis by adding the value of its current X coordinate to the value of ballXSpeed (e.g., the speed and direction the sprite is moving). Likewise, the second statement updates the sprite's location on the Y axis by adding the value of its current Y coordinate to the value of ballYSpeed. The last two statements update the X and Y coordinates of the rectangle used to display the sprite on the screen.

Detecting When Sprites Move Off the Screen

Depending on the type of games you develop, sprites may be allowed to move off of the screen such as would be the case in a game where the objective is to shoot down flying objects as they appear and move across the screen. However, in most cases you'll want to ensure that sprites remain on the screen. As such, you need to know how to detect when sprites reach the edge of the screen so that you can halt their progress and perhaps send them back in a different direction.

The following example demonstrates how to determine when a sprite reaches the right-hand side of the screen.

```
if (ballX + ballRect.Width >= graphics.GraphicsDevice.Viewport.Width)
{
    ballXSpeed = ballXSpeed * -1;
}
```

Here, a check is made to see if the sprite has reached the right edge of the viewing area by adding the width of the sprite to the sprite's X coordinate and then comparing that value to see if it is greater than or equal to the value returned by graphics.GraphicsDevice.Viewport.Width. If this is the case, the sprite's direction and speed is reversed by multiplying ballXSpeed by −1. Similarly, the following example checks to see if the sprite has reached the left-hand edge of the screen and changes its speed and direction accordingly.

```
if (ballX <= 0)
{
    ballXSpeed = ballXSpeed * -1;
}
```

The following statements demonstrate how to determine when the sprite comes into contact with the top and bottom of the display area.

```
if (ballY + ballRect.Height >= graphics.GraphicsDevice.Viewport.Height)
{
    ballYSpeed = ballYSpeed * -1;
}

if (ballY <= 0)
{
    ballYSpeed = ballYSpeed * -1;
}
```

Managing Collisions

Have ever played a computer game where you know that you shot and hit a target and yet the game ignores it? This is probably because of issues with the game's collision detection. *Collisions* occur when two objects touch one another. Collision detection is a key aspect of most computer games. When done properly, the result is a realistic and fun experience. When done poorly, it can ruin a game.

Bounded Sprites

As demonstrated in Figure 10.2, sprites are graphic images displayed using `Rectangle` objects. Here, a graphic showing a fighter jet is drawn on a solid background.

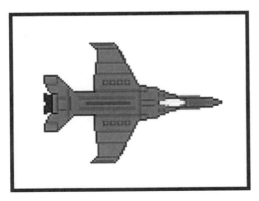

Figure 10.2
A `Rectangle` provides a sprite with a bounded container that can be used to detect collisions.

Collisions occur when two bounded sprites touch one another. Figure 10.3 shows how a typical collision looks.

`Rectangles` consist of four sets of coordinates. This makes them easy for XNA to use when detecting collisions. As such, minimal resources are consumed. This is important in situations where numerous sprites are moving about. A disadvantage of using `Rectangles` as the basis for checking for collisions is that they lack precision. As a result, XNA will sometimes detect collisions when two `Rectangles` come into contact with one another even though the images displayed within those `Rectangles` may actually just miss one another. One way of dealing with this challenge is to resize your graphic files to remove as much space as possible from the outer edges of the graphic.

Another option is to use a number of `Rectangle` objects to outline the perimeter of a sprite, as demonstrated in Figure 10.4.

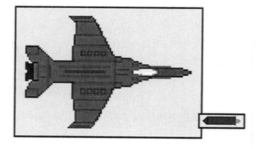

Figure 10.3
A collision occurs when the `Rectangle` objects used to display the sprites come into contact with one another.

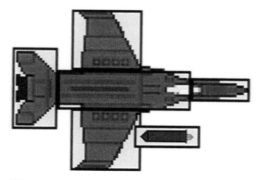

Figure 10.4
You can use multiple `Rectangles` to set up more precise collision detection.

The advantage of using this technique is that you can attain greater precision by carefully mapping out the perimeter of the sprite. The disadvantage comes in the form of greater consumption of resources, especially on a resource-constrained computer, which may adversely affect game performance.

Detecting When Collisions Occur

XNA provides a Rectangle method named Intersects() that you can use to perform collision detection. This method allows you to determine when an object comes into contact with another specified object. Its application is demonstrated here:

```
if (ballRect.Intersects(paddleRect))
{
    ballYSpeed = ballYSpeed * -1;
    collisionWave.Play();
}
```

In this example, a check is made to see if a Rectangle named ballRect has collided with a Rectangle named paddleRect. To use it, you would place it at the end of an application's Update() method.

Going Full Screen

Until now, all of the examples that you have seen have run within a window on a Windows computer. However, many games are best played in full-screen mode using a high resolution. XNA allows you to switch your game over to full-screen mode and to specify a preferred screen width and height (e.g., resolution). This is achieved using the graphics object's PreferredBackBufferWidth, Preferred-BackBufferHeight, and IsFullScreen properties, as demonstrated here:

```
public Game1()
{
    graphics = new GraphicsDeviceManager(this);

    this.graphics.PreferredBackBufferWidth = 1280;
    this.graphics.PreferredBackBufferHeight = 1024;
    this.graphics.IsFullScreen = true;

    Content.RootDirectory = "Content";
}
```

Here, a preferred resolution of 1280 × 1024 has been specified and full-screen mode is enabled by setting IsFullScreen equal to true. Note that these statements have been added to the beginning of the Game1 class and not to one of its methods.

Dealing with Display Overscan

There is one additional technical challenge known as *display overscan* that you need to be aware of if you are planning on developing games that will also run on the Xbox 360 game console. The Xbox 360 uses televisions as its display. However, there are many different types of televisions, each of which has different display features.

Televisions have a feature referred to as overscan. With overscan, televisions do not display all of an application's display. Instead, they display most of it, focusing on the center area. As a result, a small outer portion of a game's output is not displayed. Figure 10.5 depicts how overscan affects the display area that is available to your XNA games when compared to the display on your computer.

To deal with overscan and to prevent it from ruining your games by allowing critical parts of the game's area to go unseen, you should take steps to modify the display perimeter of your games, reducing it by a given percentage. To do so, you would add a variable to your application's game world data, as shown here:

```
float overScan = 12.0f;
```

Here a variable named overScan is defined and assigned a value of 12.0f, which will be used in the application to adjust the game's display area by 12 percent. Next, you need to modify the Initialize() method, as shown in bold, in order to readjust the game display area.

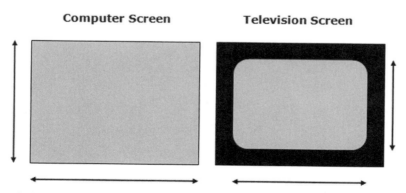

Figure 10.5
Because of overscan, you must be careful to control the display of output in your games.

```
protected override void Initialize()
{
    windowWidth = graphics.GraphicsDevice.Viewport.Width;
    windowHeight = graphics.GraphicsDevice.Viewport.Height;

    float xOverscanMargin = (windowWidth * overScan) / 100;
    float yOverscanMargin = (windowHeight * overScan) / 100;

    //Use the over scan margin to set the game's borders
    windowMinX = xOverscanMargin;
    windowMinY = yOverscanMargin;
    windowMaxX = windowWidth - xOverscanMargin;
    windowMaxY = windowHeight - yOverscanMargin;

    base.Initialize();
}
```

The third and fourth statements define variables named xOverscanMargin and yOverscanMargin. These variables are assigned a calculated value that takes either the windowWidth or windowHeight variable values and multiplies them by the overScan value (percentage) divided by 100. The next four statements assign modified coordinate values representing the game's new right, left, upper, and lower margins (utilizing 88 percent of the game's overall display area).

Of course, to be useful, you need to apply these new margins to the statements that control the movement of sprites within the game, as demonstrated here:

```
if (ballX + ballRect.Width >= windowMaxX)
{
    ballXSpeed = ballXSpeed * -1;
}
```

These statements reverse the direction of a rectangle named ballRect when it reaches the game's right-hand adjusted margin.

Creating the XNA Breakout Game

Okay, it is time to put everything you have learned together through the creation of a new XNA game called XNA Breakout. This game will support two states, using the graphic shown in Figure 10.6 as a splash screen that will manage the transition between games.

The objective of this game is for the player to keep the ball in play while scoring as many points as possible. The player has a total of three lives and must use the

Figure 10.6
The splash screen is used to give the player control over when the game is started.

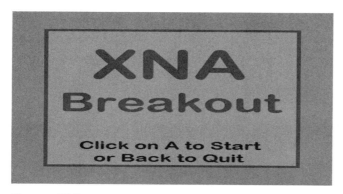

Figure 10.7
The game uses a splash screen to initiate and pause game play between rounds.

gamepad to control paddle movement. Figure 10.7 shows how the game looks when first started.

To initiate game play, the player must press the A button on the gamepad. When this happens, the game switches states and the screen shown in Figure 10.8 appears. The ball immediately begins bouncing around the screen.

Figure 10.9 shows how the game looks after a few moments of play. As you can see, several bricks have been removed and the player has been rewarded with points.

Game play ends when the player loses his third life or when the Back button on the gamepad is pressed. Due to the size and complexity of this game, it will be developed in a series of 15 steps. First you will develop the programming logic for the standard XNA game methods (i.e., `Initialize()`, `LoadContent()`, `Update()`, and `Draw()`). To keep programming logic manageable, you will break it down

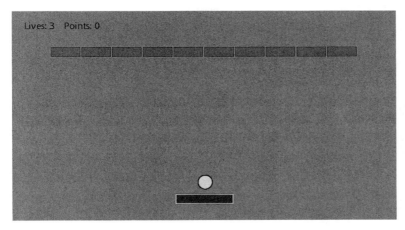

Figure 10.8
Each new point begins with the ball and paddle centered at the bottom of the screen.

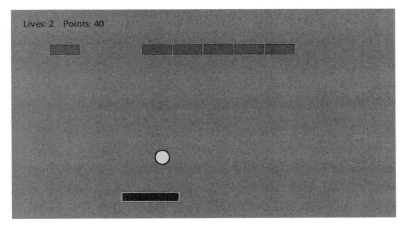

Figure 10.9
The goal of the game is for the player to keep the ball in play and to score as many points as possible.

into related units, storing it in various custom made methods. To help make things as easy as possible to understand, comments have been added throughout the program file.

Step 1—Creating a New Project

The first step in creating the XNA Breakout game is to start XNA and create a new project. Click on File > New Project. Next, select the Windows Game (3.1) template, type **XNA Breakout** in the Name field, and click on the OK button. Once created, you need to add a number of graphic and audio files to the application as well as a new font.

Importing the Audio Files

This game makes use of two audio files, one named collision.wav that is played whenever the game's ball is deflected off of the edge of the screen or when it collides with the paddle, and one named miss.wav that is played whenever the player allows the ball to drop down past the paddle. To add the collision.wav files, right-click on the Content folder located in the Solution Explorer window and click on Add > Existing Item. Then locate the audio file and click on the Add button. Repeat the above process to add the miss.wav file.

Hint

You will find copies of these two audio files as well as the game's graphic files on this book's companion website located at www.courseptr.com/downloads/.

Importing the Graphic Files

The XNA Breakout game makes use of a number of images. The images are named ball.png, paddle.png, redbrick.png, and splash.png. Add these four files to your program using the same process you followed when adding the game's audio files.

Importing and Configuring Fonts

The last piece of content that you need to add to the application is a font that will be used to display the player scores and the number of lives he has remaining. To add the font, right-click on Content and then click on Add > New Item. When the Add New Item – Content window appears, select the Sprite Font icon and click on Add. XNA will add a Sprite Font named SpriteFont1.spritefont to the project. The content of the new Sprite Font file is displayed in the code editor window. Locate and modify the <Size> tag entry, as shown here in bold:

```
<!--
Size is a float value, measured in points. Modify this value to change
the size of the font.
-->
<Size>24</Size>
```

Step 2—Defining Game World Data

Now it is time to start developing the game's programming logic. To begin, you need to define the game world data as shown next. This data include an assortment of variables that are used to manage the game screen, its sprites, audio files, and font. An array and a structure are defined that will be used to manage the display of the game's bricks. In addition, a number of other variables are defined that are used to keep track of game state, player score, etc. Lastly, a GameSpriteStruct variable is defined to support the game's splash screen.

```
public class Game1 : Microsoft.Xna.Framework.Game
{
    GraphicsDeviceManager graphics;
    SpriteBatch spriteBatch;

    //Game world data

    //Application windows data
    float windowWidth;
    float windowHeight;
    float overScan = 10.0f;
    float windowMinX;
    float windowMaxX;
    float windowMinY;
    float windowMaxY;

    //Data for the application's ball
    Texture2D ballTexture;
    Rectangle ballRect;
    float ballX;
    float ballXSpeed;
    float ballY;
    float ballYSpeed;
    float ballSize = 0.04f;

    //Data for the application's paddle
    Texture2D paddleTexture;
    Rectangle paddleRect;
    float paddleX;
    float paddleXSpeed;
    float paddleY;
    float paddleSize = 0.15f;
```

```
//Data for the application's bricks
Texture2D brickTexture;
GameSpriteStruct[] bricks;   //Define bricks array
int noOfBricks = 10;         //Number of bricks to be displayed

//These variables represent audio files
SoundEffect collisionWave;
SoundEffect missWave;

//Define variables of type Font to be used to display text
SpriteFont font;

//Various game variables
int plays = 3;               //A game consists of 3 plays
int noObVisibleBricks;       //Tracks the number of visible bricks
int playerScore = 0;         //Tracks player score
bool stateOfGame = false;    //Tracks game state
float space;                 //Used to determine space between bricks

//This structure defines data for the game's bricks
struct GameSpriteStruct
{
    public Texture2D spriteTexture;
    public Rectangle spriteRect;
    public float X;
    public float Y;
    public float WidthFactor;
    public bool Visible;
}

GameSpriteStruct splash;



    .
    .
    .
```

Step 3—Setting Screen Resolution and Full-Screen Mode

Once you have finished coding the game world data, you will need to configure the game to run in full-screen mode by modifying the Game1() method, as shown here:

```
public Game1()
{
```

```
    graphics = new GraphicsDeviceManager(this);

    this.graphics.PreferredBackBufferWidth = 1280;
    this.graphics.PreferredBackBufferHeight = 720;
    this.graphics.IsFullScreen = true;

    Content.RootDirectory = "Content";
}
```

Here, the game's resolution has been specified and it has been configured to run in full-screen mode.

Step 4—Initializing Game Play

Before the game begins running, you need to configure the initial state of the display screen. This involves a number of different tasks so rather than keying them all into the Initialize() method, you will create a new method named ConfigureScreen() and place the required programming statements there. For now, to begin setting things up, modify the Initialize() method to call on the ConfigureScreen() method.

```
protected override void Initialize()
{
    ConfigureScreen();  //This method establishes screen configuration
    base.Initialize();
}
```

Step 5—Loading Game Content

The next step in the development of the game is to load all of its content. To do so, modify the LoadContent() method as shown next. As you can see, the statement loads the game's graphics, audio files, and font. In addition, it executes several methods, which are responsible for managing the configuration of the game's ball and paddle, configuring the display of its bricks and the display of its splash screen.

```
protected override void LoadContent()
{
    //Create a new SpriteBatch, which can be used to draw textures.
    spriteBatch = new SpriteBatch(GraphicsDevice);

    //Load the game's graphic files into memory
    ballTexture = Content.Load<Texture2D>("ball");
```

```
    paddleTexture = Content.Load<Texture2D>("paddle");
    brickTexture = Content.Load<Texture2D>("redbrick");
    splash.spriteTexture = Content.Load<Texture2D>("splash");

    //Call method that configures the game's ball and paddle
    ConfigureBallAndPaddle();

    //Load the game's audio files into memory
    collisionWave = Content.Load<SoundEffect>("collision");
    missWave = Content.Load<SoundEffect>("miss");

    //Load the game's font
    font = Content.Load<SpriteFont>("SpriteFont1");

//Instantiate a bricks object
bricks = new GameSpriteStruct[noOfBricks];

ConfigureBricks();     //Call on method that configures the bricks
DisplaySplashScreen(); //Call on method that displays the splash screen
}
```

Step 6—Updating Game Play

As you would expect, Update() is responsible for managing the overall execution of the game. It begins by checking to see if the player has pressed the Back button, signaling an instruction to halt game play. Next, it retrieves gamepad state. If the A button is pressed, it calls on a method named StartGame() to initiate game play.

```
protected override void Update(GameTime gameTime)
{
    // Allows the game to exit
    if (GamePad.GetState(PlayerIndex.One).Buttons.Back ==
      ButtonState.Pressed)
    {
        this.Exit();
    }

    //Retrieve gamepad state data
    GamePadState gamePad1 = GamePad.GetState(PlayerIndex.One);

    //Start game play when the player presses the gamepad's A button
    if (gamePad1.Buttons.A == ButtonState.Pressed)
```

```
    {
        StartGame();  //This method starts game play
    }

    if (stateOfGame == true)  //A value of true indicates active game play
    {
        //Determine the paddle's location
        paddleX = paddleX + (paddleXSpeed * gamePad1.ThumbSticks.Right.X);

        ProcessPaddleMovement();
        ProcessBallMovement();
        KeepTrackOfBricks();
    }

    base.Update(gameTime);
}
```

The Update() method ends with an if statement code block that executes when the value of stateOfGame is set equal to true, signaling that game play is in progress.

Step 7—Drawing the Game

In order to display the game on the screen, you must modify the Draw() method, as shown next. The method's execution is controlled by a switch code block. It executes either of two case statements, depending on the value assigned to stateOfGame. When set to false, the game's splash screen is displayed. When set to true, game play is in progress and the game executes a series of Draw statements.

```
protected override void Draw(GameTime gameTime)
{
    GraphicsDevice.Clear(Color.CornflowerBlue);
    Vector2 textVector1 = new Vector2(40, 30);

    spriteBatch.Begin();
    switch (stateOfGame)
    {
        case false:  //A value of false means it's time to display the
                     //splash screen
            spriteBatch.Draw(splash.spriteTexture, splash.spriteRect,
              Color.White);
            break;
```

```
case true:  //A value of true indicates active game play
    //Draw the ball, paddle and score
    spriteBatch.Draw(ballTexture, ballRect, Color.White);
    spriteBatch.Draw(paddleTexture, paddleRect, Color.White);
    spriteBatch.DrawString(font, "Lives: " + plays.ToString() +
        "  Points: " + playerScore.ToString(), textVector1,
        Color.Black);

    //Draw only visible bricks
    for (int i = 0; i < noOfBricks; i++)
    {
        if (bricks[i].Visible)
        {
            spriteBatch.Draw(bricks[i].spriteTexture,
                bricks[i].spriteRect, Color.White);
        }
    }
    break;
    }
    spriteBatch.End();

    base.Draw(gameTime);
}
```

The Draw() method also draws the bricks on the screen. It does this using a loop
that iterates through the bricks array to determine which bricks are supposed to
be visible and then drawing those bricks on the screen.

Step 8—Configuring the Screen

The rest of the program file is made up of a collection of custom methods, each of
which is designed to perform a specific task. The first of these methods is the
ConfigureScreen() method shown next. This method is called by the Initi-
alize() method. It begins by retrieving the screen's dimensions. It then uses the
information to calculate the game's overscan margin, after which it determines
the right, left, upper, and lower boundaries for the game. It also positions the
player's paddle at the bottom of the screen, 20 pixels above its lower boundary.

```
//This method establishes screen configuration
private void ConfigureScreen()
{
    //Set window width and height
```

```
windowWidth = graphics.GraphicsDevice.Viewport.Width;
windowHeight = graphics.GraphicsDevice.Viewport.Height;

//Calculate the over scan margin (for Xbox 360)
float xOverscanMargin = (windowWidth * overScan) / 100;
float yOverscanMargin = (windowHeight * overScan) / 100;

//Use the over scan margin to set the game's borders
windowMinX = xOverscanMargin;
windowMinY = yOverscanMargin;
windowMaxX = windowWidth - xOverscanMargin;
windowMaxY = windowHeight - yOverscanMargin;

//Position the paddle at the bottom of the window
paddleY = windowMaxY - 20;
}
```

Step 9—Configuring the Ball and Paddle

The ConfigureBallAndPaddle() method, shown next, is initially called by the LoadContent() method and later by the ProcessBallMovement() method. It is responsible for adjusting the size of the game's ball and paddle and assigning their starting location. The ball and paddle's speeds are also configured.

```
//This method configures sprite width and height and paddle location
void ConfigureBallAndPaddle()
{
    //Set ball size
    ballRect.Width = (int)((windowWidth * ballSize) + 0.5f);
    float ratio = (float)ballTexture.Width / ballTexture.Height;
    ballRect.Height = (int)((ballRect.Width / ratio) + 0.5f);

    //Position the ball at the bottom center of the window just
    //above the paddle
    ballY = windowMaxY - 80;
    ballX = (windowWidth - ballRect.Width) / 2;

    ballXSpeed = windowWidth / 140.0f;      //Set ball's horizontal speed
    ballYSpeed = ballXSpeed * -1;           //Set ball's vertical speed

    //Set paddle size
    paddleRect.Width = (int)((windowWidth * paddleSize) + 0.5f);
```

```
    ratio = (float)paddleTexture.Width / paddleTexture.Height;
    paddleRect.Height = (int)((paddleRect.Width / ratio) + 0.5f);

    //Position the paddle at the bottom center of the window
    paddleX = (windowWidth - paddleRect.Width) / 2;

    paddleXSpeed = windowWidth / 100.0f;  //Set speed the paddle can move
}
```

Step 10—Starting Game Play

The StartGame() method, shown next, is called by the Update() method and is responsible for resetting the values assigned to several game variables in order to set up a new game. In addition, it calls upon a method named ConfigureBricks(), which will configure the display of a fresh set of bricks at the top of the screen.

```
//This method starts game play
private void StartGame()
{
    stateOfGame = true; //A value of true initiates game play
    plays = 3;          //Reset the player's lives
    playerScore = 0;    //Reset the player's score

    ConfigureBricks();  //This method reconfigures a new screen of bricks
}
```

Step 11—Processing Player Input

The ProcessPaddleMovement() method, shown next, is called by the Update() method and is responsible for keeping track of the location of the paddle on the screen and for making sure that its movement is restricted to the game's display area (i.e., to prevent it from moving off the screen).

```
//This method handles the movement of the paddle
private void ProcessPaddleMovement()
{
    paddleRect.X = (int)paddleX;  //Set the paddle's horizontal location
    paddleRect.Y = (int)paddleY;  //Set the paddle's vertical location

    //Halt paddle when it reaches the right edge of the display area
    if (paddleX + paddleRect.Width >= windowMaxX)
    {
```

```
        paddleRect.X = (int)windowMaxX - paddleRect.Width;
    }

    //Halt paddle when it reaches the left edge of the display area
    if (paddleX <= windowMinX) paddleRect.X = (int)windowMinX;
}
```

Step 12—Managing Ball Movement

The `ProcessBallMovement()` method, shown next, is called by the `Update()` method and is responsible for bouncing the ball around the screen. It also keeps track of player lives and sets the value of `startOfgame` to `false` when the player runs out of lives.

```
//This method handles the movement of the ball
private void ProcessBallMovement()
{
    //Determine the ball's location
    ballX = ballX + ballXSpeed;
    ballY = ballY + ballYSpeed;

    ballRect.X = (int)(ballX + 0.5f); //Set the ball's horizontal location
    ballRect.Y = (int)(ballY + 0.5f); //Set the ball's vertical location

    //Reverse ball direction along the X-axis when it reaches the right
    //hand side of the display area
    if (ballX + ballRect.Width >= windowMaxX)
    {
        ballXSpeed = ballXSpeed * -1;
        collisionWave.Play();              //Play sound effect
    }

    //Reverse ball direction along the X-axis when it reaches the
    //left hand side of the display area
    if (ballX <= windowMinX)
    {
        ballXSpeed = ballXSpeed * -1;
        collisionWave.Play();              //Play sound effect
    }

    //Halt the current round of play if the ball reaches the bottom
    //of the display area
```

```
        if (ballY + ballRect.Height >= windowMaxY)
        {
            missWave.Play();              //Play sound effect
            plays = plays - 1;            //Take away one of the player's lives
            ConfigureBallAndPaddle();

            //Mark the game as over when the player lives are gone
            if (plays == 0) stateOfGame = false;
        }

        //Reverse ball direction along the Y axis when the ball reaches the
        //top of the display area
        if (ballY <= windowMinY)
        {
            ballYSpeed = ballYSpeed * -1;
            collisionWave.Play();                 //Play sound effect
        }

        //Reverse ball direction along the Y axis when it collides
        //with the paddle
        if (ballRect.Intersects(paddleRect))
        {
            ballYSpeed = ballYSpeed * -1;
            collisionWave.Play();                 //Play sound effect
        }
    }
}
```

Step 13—Keeping Track of the Bricks

The KeepTrackOfBricks() method, shown next, is called by the Update() method and is responsible for managing collisions between the bricks and the ball. It uses a for loop to iterate through every brick in the game in order to check for a collision. If the ball collides with a block that is visible, the ball is deflected back and the brick is made invisible. If the ball collides with an invisible block, the collision is ignored and the ball is allowed to continue on its way.

```
//This method manages the game's bricks
private void KeepTrackOfBricks()
{
    //Iterate once for every brick
    for (int i = 0; i < noOfBricks; i++)
    {
```

```
    //Check to see if the brick is visible
    if (bricks[i].Visible)
    {
        //Process a collision between the ball and a brick
        if (ballRect.Intersects(bricks[i].spriteRect))
        {
            bricks[i].Visible = false;  //Mark the brick as invisible
            noObVisibleBricks = noObVisibleBricks - 1; //Update count
            playerScore = playerScore + 10;   //Increase player score
            ballYSpeed = ballYSpeed * -1;  //Reverse ball movement
            collisionWave.Play();           //Play sound effect
            break;  //Exit the loop
        }
    }

    //Set the X and Y coordinates for the brick
    bricks[i].spriteRect.X = (int)bricks[i].X;
    bricks[i].spriteRect.Y = (int)bricks[i].Y;
}

//If there are no more bricks left then redisplay them
if (noObVisibleBricks == 0) ConfigureBricks();
}
```

This method is also responsible for keeping track of the player's score, adding 10 points to it for every brick that is hit. This method also redisplays all of the bricks by calling on the ConfigureBricks() method as soon as the last brick is cleared from the screen in order to give the player an endless stream of new bricks to knock out.

Step 14—Redisplaying the Bricks

The ConfigureBricks() method, shown next, is initially called by the LoadContent() method and later called by the StartGame() and KeepTrackOfBricks() methods. It is responsible for displaying a fresh set of bricks on the screen.

```
//This method configures the display of red bricks across the top
//of the game window
private void ConfigureBricks()
{
    //Calculate the spacing between the bricks
    space = (windowMaxX - windowMinX) / noOfBricks;
```

```
//Set variable equal to the total number of bricks
noObVisibleBricks = noOfBricks;

//This loop populates the bricks array with bricks, configures them,
//and marks them as visible
for (int i = 0; i < noOfBricks; i++)
{
    bricks[i].spriteTexture = brickTexture;
    bricks[i].WidthFactor = 0.08f;
    bricks[i].spriteRect.Width = (int)((windowWidth * 0.08f) + 0.5f);
    float ratio = (float)bricks[i].spriteTexture.Width /
      bricks[i].spriteTexture.Height;
    bricks[i].spriteRect.Height = (int)((bricks[i].spriteRect.Width /
      ratio) + 0.5f);
    bricks[i].X = windowMinX + (i * space);
    bricks[i].Y = windowMinY + 50;
    bricks[i].Visible = true;
}
}
```

Step 15—Displaying the Splash Screen

The last of the game's custom methods is the `DisplaySplashScreen()` method, shown next. This method is called by the `LoadContent()` method and is responsible for displaying the game's splash screen when the game is initially started.

```
//This method displays the game's splash screen
private void DisplaySplashScreen()
{
    //Display the game's splash screen
    splash.spriteRect = new Rectangle((int)windowMinX, (int)windowMinY,
      (int)(windowMaxX - windowMinX), (int)(windowMaxY - windowMinY));
}
```

Okay, that's everything you need to finish up your copy of the XNA Breakout game. Go ahead and try it out. Assuming you followed along carefully with the instructions that were provided, everything should work as advertised. Before you move on to the final chapter, you might consider taking a few minutes to make the XNA Breakout game even better. For example, consider modifying the game to make it harder to play the longer the player is able to keep the ball in play by slightly increasing the ball speed every time the player deflects it back.

H i n t

In the event you don't have time to re-create your own copy of the XNA Breakout game from scratch, you can always download a working copy of the game from this book's companion website, located at www.courseptr.com/downloads.

Also, you might want to give the player a bonus life if he can reach a certain score level. Alternatively, you might consider shrinking the size of the paddle over time to make it harder for the player to hit the ball. By making the game progressively more difficult to play, you can make the game more fun and challenging.

Summary

In this chapter you learned about a host of different programming techniques, enabling you to do things like manage game state and add a splash screen to your games. You learned how to manage sprite size appropriately and to ensure that your sprites retain their proper appearance. In addition, this chapter showed you how to control the movement of sprites on the screen and how to perform collision detection. To help tie all of these programming concepts together, this chapter ended by guiding you through the creation of your first real computer game.

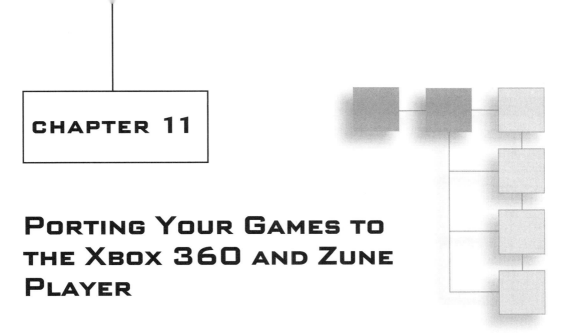

CHAPTER 11

PORTING YOUR GAMES TO THE XBOX 360 AND ZUNE PLAYER

Welcome to this book's final chapter. Now that you have learned how to program using C#, as well as the fundamental steps involved in developing games using Microsoft XNA, it is time to address issues involved in deploying your games to Xbox 360 and the Zune player. After all, the ability to create games for a next-generation game console and media player is probably one of the main reasons you are interested in XNA. You will also learn how to submit your XNA games for peer review to the XNA Creators Club Online website, where if they are approved, your games will then be made available for sale on the Xbox Live Marketplace. In addition to all this, this chapter will also discuss how to deal with program errors and how to debug your XNA applications.

An overview of the major topics covered in this chapter includes learning how to:

- Customize and deploy your XNA games to Xbox 360 and the Zune player

- Create platform-specific games and convert games from one platform to another

- Debug your XNA applications using breakpoints and step through program execution

- Create exception handlers that can handle specific and general types of runtime errors

Deploying Your XNA Games to Other Platforms

Up to this point in the book, the primary focus has been on learning how to develop games and run them on your computer. But it's XNA's ability to support game development for Xbox 360 and the Zune player that really make it stand out from other game development frameworks. Until XNA came along, the development of games for media players and game consoles was pretty much the exclusive domain of professional programmers. Now all that has changed. Even better is the fact that Microsoft now provides XNA developers with the opportunity to submit their games for peer review when they become members of the XNA Creators Club. Games that pass the review are made available to the Xbox community via the Xbox Live Marketplace. This provides you with access to a global market of game enthusiasts. How cool is that?

Setting Up Connections

In order to port your XNA games from your computer to your Zune player or Xbox 360, you must establish a connection between them. This is done using the XNA Game Studio Device Center. Instructions for setting up these connections was provided in Chapter 2. Once you have established connections to these devices, assuming you have both, you should see them listed in the XNA Games Studio Device Center window, as demonstrated in Figure 11.1.

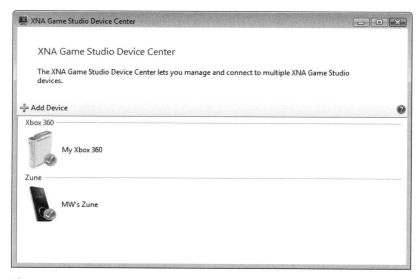

Figure 11.1
An example of a computer with connections to both an Xbox 360 and a Zune player.

Developing Cross-Platform Games

The most common approach to developing games for the Xbox 360 and the Zune player is to create your games and get them working correctly on your computer and then to port them over to other platforms, adding platform-specific features and code adjustments. A big reason this approach works so well is that between 95 and 100 percent of your program code will work just fine with no changes required. However, sometimes you will have to make changes or additions to your code. The primary purpose of this chapter is to identify these types of situations and to provide you with guidance on what you will need to do. If you prefer, you may of course start out developing a game for a specific platform without first generating a Windows version.

Creating a Platform-Specific Game

If you only want to create a game for a specific platform, you can do so by clicking on File > New Project and then selecting either Xbox 360 Game (3.1) or Zune Game (3.1) from the available list of new project templates, as shown in Figure 11.2.

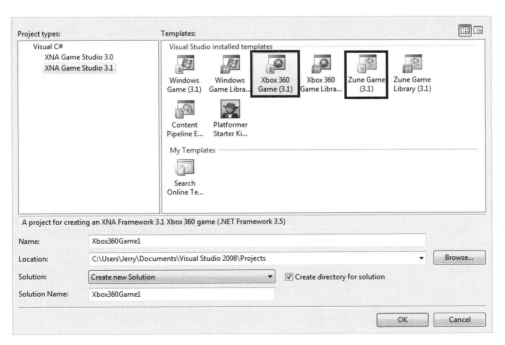

Figure 11.2
Creating a platform-specific game.

Next, enter a name for the game and then click on OK. In response, XNA will create a new project for you. It will include all of the expected methods (`Initialize()`, `LoadContent()`, `UnloadContent()`, `Update()` and `Draw()`). At this point, you can go ahead and begin developing your game.

Hint

There is one small difference between the code that is automatically generated for a Zune game and that of a Windows or Xbox game. Specifically, an extra comment and code statement is included in the `Game1` class defined at the beginning of the program file in Zune games, as shown next in bold.

```
public Game1()
{
    graphics = new GraphicsDeviceManager(this);
    Content.RootDirectory = "Content";

    // Frame rate is 30 fps by default for Zune.
    TargetElapsedTime = TimeSpan.FromSeconds(1 / 30.0);
}
```

Remember, the Zune player redraws its screen at a default rate of 30 frames per second, not 60 like on Windows and the Xbox 360.

Converting a Windows Game to Another Platform

Although you can start out creating a game for a specific platform as just described, a more commonly used approach is to start out creating your game for your computer. Once you have the core of the game developed and have tested and debugged any problems that may have occurred, most XNA developers then create a copy of the game for either Xbox 360 or the Zune player (or both) and then finish up by making any needed platform-specific adjustments to the game.

When you follow this Windows development first approach to game development, you will have a single project to manage as you begin game development, as shown in Figure 11.3.

Once you have the game up and running properly on your computer, you can make a copy of it for the desired target platform by right-clicking on the project name in Solution Explorer, as shown in Figure 11.4, and selecting either Create Copy of Project for Xbox 360 or Create Copy of Project for Zune.

Hint

Note that if you began game development by creating a project for either the Xbox 360 or the Zune player, you would see an option to Create Copy of Project for Windows.

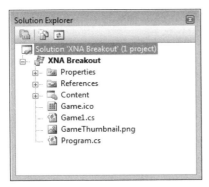

Figure 11.3
An XNA game made up of a single project.

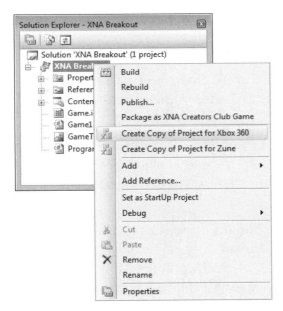

Figure 11.4
Creating a copy of a game for the Xbox 360.

Once done, a second copy of your project will be added to Solution Explorer, as demonstrated in Figure 11.5. The new copy of your game project contains a complete copy of all of the files that make up the original project.

Note that any changes you make to one project are also made to the other project. Therefore, if you create a project for Windows, then make a copy of the project for Xbox 360, and then make a change to the Xbox 360 copy of the project, the changes are made in both the Windows and the Xbox 360 project. You can work

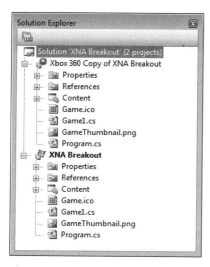

Figure 11.5
An XNA project with code for both Windows and Xbox 360.

around this restriction by embedding platform-specific code statements inside conditional compilation symbols, as discussed later in this chapter.

Also note that when working with multiple projects, only one project at a time can be set as the startup project. This is the project that is compiled and executed when you run your game from within the IDE. To specify which project you want to make the startup project, right-click on the project name and select Set as Startup Project, as demonstrated in Figure 11.6.

Once you have specified which project should be the startup project and are ready to test its execution on the target platform, click on Debug > Start Debug, and XNA will attempt to compile the application. If compilation is successful, it will connect to and install the project on the specified target platform (assuming that you have connected the target device to your computer and that it is powered on and ready to go).

Trap

To connect to and deploy an application to a Zune player, add the device to your computer using the XNA Game Studio Device Center as was explained in Chapter 2. Don't forget to make sure your Zune player is turned on. To connect and deploy to Xbox 360 you must start the XNA Creators Club software on your Xbox 360 to put the device into connection mode and add the device to your computer using the XNA Game Studio Device Center.

Once deployed, your XNA game will automatically start on the specified target platform. Since the game is installed on the target platform, you can play it

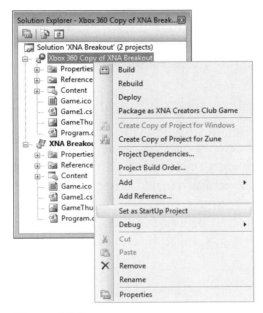

Figure 11.6
Setting a project as the startup project.

whenever you wish. On the Zune you will access it from the Games menu. On the Xbox 360 you will access it by opening the Xbox Game Library.

Platform Issues to Consider

Okay, so now you know how to create platform-specific applications and how to convert applications from one platform to another. You also know how to deploy your XNA games to Xbox 360 and the Zune player. Now it's time to consider different platform issues that you need to address to ensure that your games will run just as well on the Xbox 360 and Zune player as they do on your Windows computer.

Hint

If you implement the programming techniques covered in Chapter 10 that address cross-platform management of sprite size and shape, screen overscan, and screen resolution and size, you will significantly reduce the complexity and challenges involved in converting your XNA games from one platform to another.

Differences in Input

One primary difference in game support across Windows, Xbox 360, and the Zune player is the management of input. Windows games can use a mouse, a keyboard, and a gamepad controller. Xbox 360's primary input device is the gamepad. However, if you attach a USB keyboard to it, the Xbox 360 will work with it. If your XNA games make use of the mouse as an input device, you must rework them to use either the keyboard or gamepad instead if you want them to work with the Xbox 360.

To complicate matters further, the Zune player does not support the mouse or keyboard, and although its controls map to the gamepad, it only supports a subset of the gamepad's controls. To complicate things still further, the way the Zune maps its controls to the gamepad depends on whether you are working with a first- or second-generation player. Specifically, first-generation players respond to Zune pad (Dpad) input, whereas second-generation players respond to both Dpad and left thumbstick input. When processing Zune pad (Dpad) input for either a first- or second-generation Zune player, binary data is received as shown here:

```
if (GamePad.GetState(PlayerIndex.One).Dpad.Up == ButtonState.Pressed)
{
    //The player wants to move up
}
if (GamePad.GetState(PlayerIndex.One).Dpad.Down == ButtonState.Pressed)
{
    //The player wants to move down
}
if (GamePad.GetState(PlayerIndex.One).Dpad.Left == ButtonState.Pressed)
{
    //The player wants to move left
}
if (GamePad.GetState(PlayerIndex.One).Dpad.Right == ButtonState.Pressed)
{
    //The player wants to move right
}
```

On the other hand, second-generation Zune players also map Zune pad input to the gamepad's left thumbstick, providing X and Y coordinate data. As such, you could process Dpad input as shown here:

```
paddleX = paddleX + (paddleXSpeed * gamePad1.ThumbSticks.Left.X);
paddleY = paddleY + (paddleYSpeed * gamePad1.ThumbSticks.Left.Y);
```

Hint

Refer to Chapter 7 for additional input on how XNA maps the Zune player's controls to the gamepad's controls.

Unlike a Windows computer or an Xbox 360, the Zune player does not support the use of multiple controllers. As such, you must always use `PlayerIndex.One` when retrieving game input. For example, to determine if the player has pressed the Zune player's Zune pad control, which maps to the gamepad's A button, you would execute the following statement.

```
if (GamePad.GetState(PlayerIndex.One).Buttons.A == ButtonState.Pressed)
{
    //The A button has been pressed
}
```

Audio Compatibility

As you learned in Chapter 9, XNA supports the integration of audio in XNA games through either the Cross-Platform Audio Creation Tool (XACT) or its new API. If you elected to work with XACT and you only create games for Windows or Xbox 360, you are good to go. However, if you later decide to convert your game to the Zune player, you must convert all audio to work with the API.

The API is a simple tool but is sufficient to play both background music and audio effects. As long as you use it in your games, as explained in Chapter 9, you should not have to convert or make any changes to the code statements that manage your game's audio.

Trick

In addition to playing the audio files that you add to your application's content pipeline, you can also play songs stored in your Zune player's media library. To do so, add the following statements to your XNA application.

```
MediaLibrary zuneLib = new MediaLibrary();
SongCollection songList = zuneLib.Songs;
MediaPlayer.Play(songList);
```

This example will also work on a Windows computer where a Zune player and the Zune software have been installed.

Handling Different Screen Sizes and Resolution

Another issue that you need to keep in mind when creating cross-platform games is screen size and resolution. In Chapter 10, you were shown an example of how to develop applications that automatically calculate and adjust the size of their graphics based on the width and height of the displays being used by the systems they run on. This developmental approach is highly recommended.

If you elect not to apply this technique in your games, then you will need to address it programmatically within your program code. To do this, you will have to make use of conditional compilation symbols. You will learn about conditional compilation symbols and see an example of how to use them to adjust screen size in the next section.

Conditional Compilation

As has already been noted, XNA allows you to add platform-specific programming logic by embedding code statements within conditional compilation symbols. A conditional compilation symbol is a set of characters that mark a set of code statements that are indented for specific platforms. As such, only statements applicable to a given platform are compiled into a specific platform's copy of your XNA game.

XNA automatically defines default conditional compilation symbols for each platform that you add to your XNA projects. To view the conditional compilation symbols for an Xbox 360 version of a project, click on Project > Xbox 360 Copy of *Xxxxxx* Properties (where *Xxxxxx* is the name of the game). In response, the screen shown in Figure 11.7 is opened in the code editor window.

As shown in Figure 11.7, XNA generates two conditional compilation symbols for Xbox 360 that are used to mark platform-specific program code. These symbols are XBOX and XBOX360 respectively. XNA generates a single conditional compilation symbol for both the Zune and Windows. These are the ZUNE and WINDOWS symbols.

The following example demonstrates how to use conditional compilation symbols to adjust an application's screen size.

```
#if !ZUNE
    graphics.PreferredBackBufferHeight = 600;
    graphics.PreferredBackBufferWidth = 800;
#else
    graphics.PreferredBackBufferHeight = 320;
    graphics.PreferredBackBufferWidth = 240;
#endif
```

In this example, a screen size of 600 × 800 is used if the game is compiled for Windows or the Xbox 360 and a screen size of 320 × 240 is used if the game is compiled for execution on the Zune player.

Conditional compilation
symbols

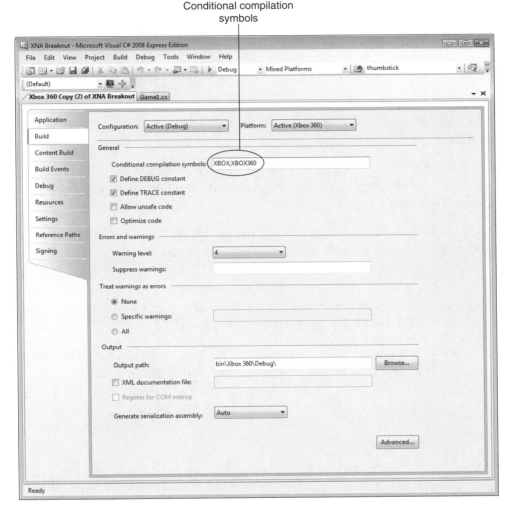

Figure 11.7
Viewing the conditional compilation symbols for Xbox 360.

Submitting Your Games to the XNA Creators Club

If, after creating an XNA game, you think it is worthy of being made available for sale on the Xbox Live Marketplace, then you need to create an XNA package for the game and submit it to the XNA Creators Club where it will undergo a thorough peer review, and, if it is approved, will be made available for sale on the Xbox Live Marketplace.

Hint

In order to submit games to the XNA Creators Club, you must sign up for the XNA Creators Club Online website and pay for a premium membership. Signing up for the XNA Creators Club and setting up a premium membership was discussed in Chapter 1.

To submit your XNA game, you must package it into a .ccgame file. This package keeps your source code and content private while letting other XNA developers play the game.

To create a .ccgame file for a finished game, begin by creating a Release version of the game. To do so, click on Build > Configuration Manager. This will display the Configuration Manager window shown in Figure 11.8.

Next, click on the Active solution configuration drop-down list and select the Release option. Make sure the Build check box is selected for the Xbox 360 copy of your game and click on Close. Now compile your game by clicking on the Green Start Debugging button on the IDE toolbar. Next, in Solution Explorer, right-click on the Xbox 360 version of the application and click on the Package as XNA Creators Club Game option, as demonstrated in Figure 11.9.

This will generate a .ccgame file for your game. To locate the file, open Windows Explorer and navigate to the folder where you saved the game. Open that folder and you will see a couple files and another folder. Drill down into the folder.

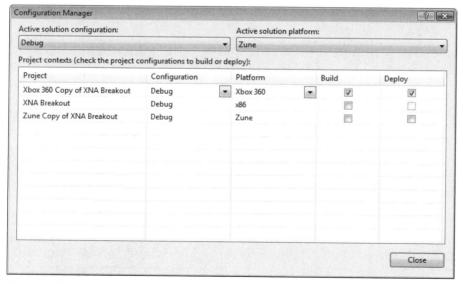

Figure 11.8
Creating a Release version of your XNA game.

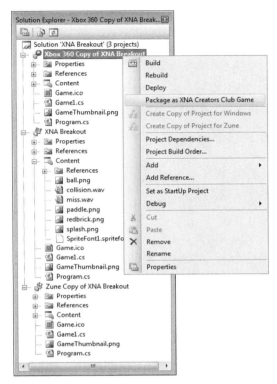

Figure 11.9
Creating a .ccgame file for your Xbox 360 game.

A number of files and folders should appear. Open the folder named bin and when in this folder drill down into the Xbox 360 folder. Locate the folder named Release and open it. The contents of this folder should resemble those shown in Figure 11.10.

The folder whose name ends with .ccgame is the folder that you will need to submit to the XNA Creators Club Online website. You may want to copy this file to a convenient location, such as your desktop, so that it will be easy to access during the submission process.

Hint

It is essential that the game you are submitting runs perfectly and that it contains no errors. If it does, do not submit it and go back and keep working on it until all errors have been eliminated.

At this point you are ready to begin the submission process. To do so, open your browser and go to http://creators.xna.com/en-US/, as shown in Figure 11.11.

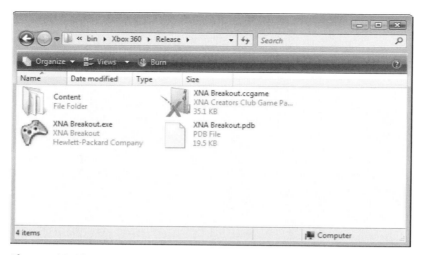

Figure 11.10
Locating the .ccgame file for your Xbox 360 game.

Figure 11.11
You submit your XNA game for peer review at the XNA Creators Club Online website.

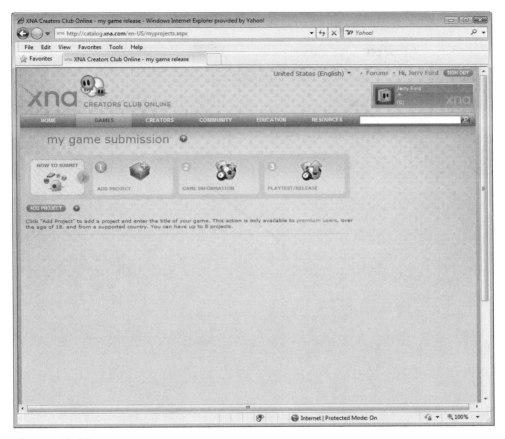

Figure 11.12
Submission of your game is a four-step process.

Next, click on Games > Submit Game. Log in using your developers account and password when prompted. The screen shown in Figure 11.12 is then displayed.

Click on the Add Project button to begin the submission process. The screen shown in Figure 11.13 appears, prompting you to enter a title for your game.

Enter a title for your game in the game title field and when ready click on Done. A new project for your game is then generated and the title you entered is displayed on the screen. To continue, click on the Add Game button. The screen shown in Figure 11.14 is then displayed.

You are prompted to supply various categories of information about your game. Begin by specifying the genre that best matches your game. Then provide a game

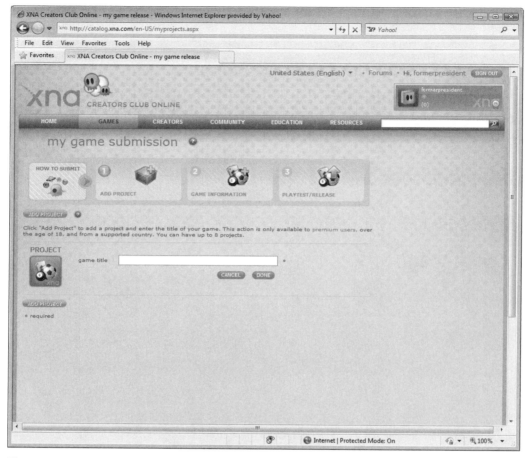

Figure 11.13
Enter a title for your XNA game.

description and provide the required classification information and supply the required media. The media needed includes things like screen prints of your game. Fill in all the required information and click on the Done button. The screen shown in Figure 11.15 is then displayed.

Here you are required to upload your game package by clicking on the upload new game binary link and then the browse link, which displays a window that you can use to locate the .ccgame file on your computer. Once selected, click on the Upload button to upload the file. Scroll down and specify a suggested price for your game and then select the countries to which it should be made

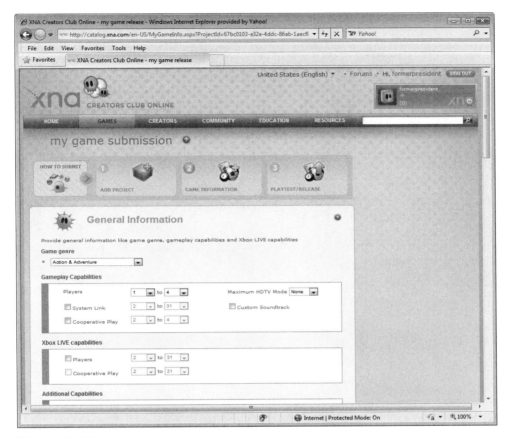

Figure 11.14
You must now answer various questions about your game.

available. Enter a few comments in the Forums Comments text field. Lastly, select either Playtest or Release. Selecting Playtest means that your game will be made available for a week to premium members on the XNA CCO website after which time you can make changes to your game based on developer feedback. Selecting Release posts your game and makes it ready for peer review. When done filling out this screen, click on the Submit button to complete the submission process.

If all goes well with the peer review process, your game will be approved and made available on Xbox Live Marketplace. If it fails to pass the peer review, you can return later and resubmit it after making any needed changes and improvements.

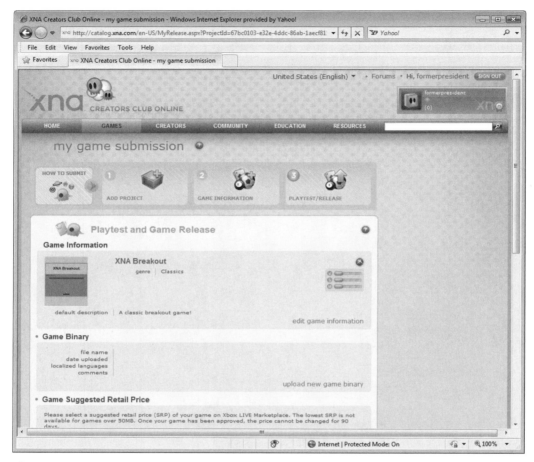

Figure 11.15
Wrapping up your submission.

Learning How to Handle Errors

As your XNA applications grow more complex, you are going to run into errors. XNA applications are subject to different types of errors that cause games to behave inappropriately. These errors are sometimes referred to as bugs. Your job is to find and remove these bugs.

To minimize the number of errors in your games you should always begin development by taking time to plan the overall design of your application. Then you can begin coding. Once finished, test your games and look for and fix any bugs. Other practices you should follow include:

- Providing players with clear instructions

- Creating an easy-to-use interface

- Using consistent naming schemes for variables, arrays, classes, and methods

- Validating user input before accepting it

- Anticipating errors and dealing with them programmatically

XNA applications are subject to three basic types of errors. These are syntax errors, logical errors, and runtime errors.

Syntax Errors

The most common error you will come across is syntax errors. Syntax errors occur when code statements fail to conform to C#'s rules. They often result from typos, such as when you mistype a keyword or omit a required parameter.

The Visual Studio Express IDE highlights syntax errors in your program code by underlining them, as demonstrated in Figure 11.16. This makes them easy to locate and fix. Syntax errors are also visible in the Error List window, as seen at the bottom of Figure 11.16. This window is automatically displayed if you try to run an XNA application with syntax errors. Each error message includes a description of the error and shows the line number of the statement that generated the error. If you double-click on an error, the IDE will locate the statement where it resides.

Trick

Sometimes you might miss when the IDE flags a syntax error in your code. To help prevent this from happening, you might want to keep the Error List window open while you are writing code. You can do this by clicking on View > Error List.

Logical Errors

A logical error is caused by a mistake on your part. For example, suppose you write a statement that adds two numbers together that you really meant to subtract. As far as XNA is concerned everything is okay. However, the output won't be what you want.

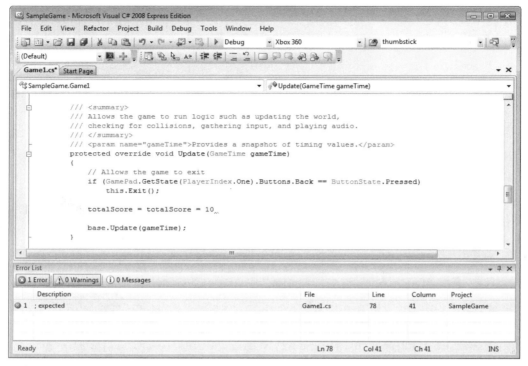

Figure 11.16
The compiler highlights syntax errors by underlining them.

The IDE cannot identify logical errors for you. The best way to prevent them is to take a little extra time to plan and formulate your program logic. Also, make sure you organize your applications into methods and that you limit your methods to specific tasks. Also set aside plenty of time to test.

Runtime Errors

A third type of error is a runtime error. These errors occur when a statement tries to do something that is impossible. For example, a runtime error will occur if your game performs an illegal operation like dividing a number by zero.

The compiler won't flag a runtime error. You have to compile your game, run it, and then do something to make the code containing the runtime error execute in order to find it. As such, runtime errors can easily be missed if you do not take the time to test your XNA games, in which case players will be left to discover your runtime errors, which is the last thing any game developer wants to let happen.

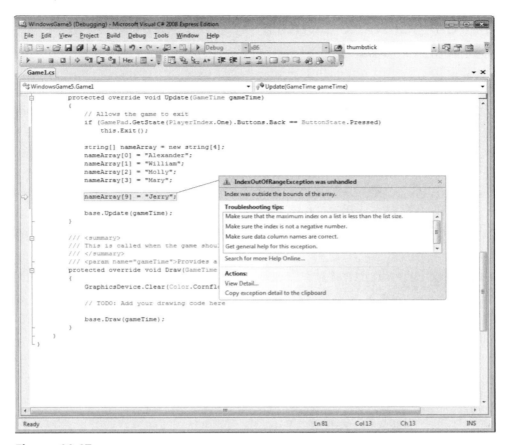

Figure 11.17
An example of a runtime error message.

If you come across a runtime error when testing an XNA application, you'll get an error message like the one shown in Figure 11.17. If you fail to find and fix a runtime error during testing, the release version of your game may or may not display an error message when it executes. Instead, it might simply stop responding or even lock up the player's computer.

Runtime errors can occur if the player provides your game unanticipated input, especially if keyboard input is involved. It is essential that you add logic to your applications that validates user input whenever possible. Unfortunately, there is no way to completely do away with runtime errors. Sometimes hardware fails or networks crash. If your game needs access to these resources, a runtime error will occur. Fortunately, as you will soon learn, you can create exception handlers that can recover from or gracefully respond to unavoidable runtime errors.

Using Breakpoints to Control Application Execution

The Visual Studio Express IDE has tools that can help you find errors. These tools will allow you to monitor code statements as they execute. You can also examine variable and property values and observe execution flow while your application executes. To work with these tools, you need to run your application in break mode.

Break mode lets you pause application execution in order to examine its status. You can use this capability to track down and locate statements that may be incorrectly setting variable or property values. In break mode you step through program code a line at a time in order to see what methods are being called and to monitor variable and property values.

Establishing Breakpoints

To configure a breakpoint in your application, locate the line where you want to place it and then click on the left-hand margin of the code editor beside the line. Once set, a circular marker is displayed in the margin. In addition, the specified line of code is highlighted, as demonstrated in Figure 11.18.

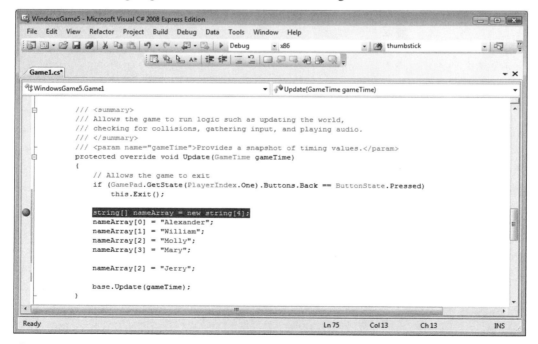

Figure 11.18
Adding a breakpoint to your application.

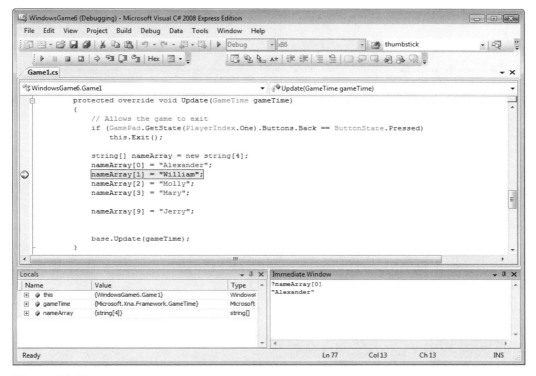

Figure 11.19
The IDE highlights the active breakpoint.

You should place breakpoints within your applications at places where you suspect problems. There is no limit to the number of breakpoints you can set. When you run your application execution pauses when a breakpoint is reached. In addition, the breakpoint's circular marker changes to an arrow, as demonstrated in Figure 11.19.

Trick

Once you have found and fixed your application's errors and no longer need the breakpoints, you can remove them. All you have to do is click on the circular markers and they'll go away.

You can gain a lot of insight into the execution of your application by establishing a breakpoint and examining property and variable values. As an example, look at the bottom of Figure 11.19 where you will see that the Locals and Immediate windows are displayed. The Locals window displays values and their type. If you want, you can modify a variable's value in the Locals window to see what effect this has on the application.

Trick

If the Locals and Immediate windows are not automatically opened, you can display them yourself by clicking on Debug > Windows > Locals and Debug > Windows > Immediate.

You can use the Immediate window to examine any variable, array, or property value. If you look at Figure 11.19, you will see that the value assigned to `name-Array[0]` was checked entering a question mark followed by the array's name and the index position of its first item.

Stepping through Application Execution

Another important debugging feature provided by the IDE is the ability to step through the execution of program statements. This way you can set a breakpoint at a section of code where you suspect an error and then step through the execution of statements that follow the breakpoint a line at a time.

The Visual Studio IDE supports three different ways of stepping through program code, as listed here:

- **Step Into.** Once halted at a breakpoint, this option executes the next statement and pauses execution

- **Step Over.** Executes entire methods pausing before the execution of the next method

- **Step Out.** Used inside a method to return to the calling statement where execution is paused again

You can switch between these three options as needed when debugging an application. The easiest way to work with these options is to click on their icons located in the IDE's standard toolbar, as shown in Figure 11.20.

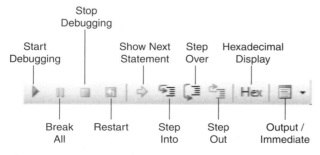

Figure 11.20
The debug icons give you control over application execution when debugging your applications.

Edit and Continue

If you find a statement with an error when debugging, the usual thing to do is stop the debugging session and fix the error, after which you can execute the application again to see the result of your changes. However, Visual Studio Express has a feature called Edit and Continue that lets you apply changes to the application when paused at a breakpoint. You can then resume execution to see what effect your change had.

To execute this feature, locate the yellow arrow that identifies the next statement to be executed and place your cursor over it. A transparent arrow will appear. Drag and drop the yellow arrow to a previous location in your program. This way you can resume execution from a previously executed statement. You can now apply your correction and click on the Step Into button to resume execution and see if the change fixed things.

Developing Exception Handlers

Runtime errors or *exceptions* occur for all kinds of reasons. Whenever possible, you should design your applications to handle unexpected exceptions without crashing or displaying cryptic error messages that are sure to confound players.

To handle exceptions, you need to locate places in your applications where errors are likely and then develop code to handle the problem. If you create an application that is subject to an error due to player input, you should add code that validates the input before accepting it. There are numerous ways of dealing with exceptions, including:

- Providing additional instruction to players

- Rewording cryptic error messages

- Requesting the player report errors

- Apologizing for errors and then closing down the application

C# supports the use of structured exception handlers as a means of preventing exceptions from creating havoc in your applications.

Structured Exception Handlers

Microsoft's recommended approach to developing exception handlers is the `try...catch...finally` code block. It allows you to enclose statements where errors may occur and then to handle them.

To set up a try...catch...finally code block, place statements where you think an exception might occur inside the try block and then add programming logic to handle the exception in the catch block. If more than one exception is possible you can add additional catch blocks, each designed for a different type of exception. You can also include an optional finally block. If included, this block will always execute even if an exception does not occur or even if a catch block executes. The finally block always executes last.

To better understand how to work with the try...catch...finally code block, let's look at the example shown here:

```
protected override void Update(GameTime gameTime)
{
    // Allows the game to exit
    if (GamePad.GetState(PlayerIndex.One).Buttons.Back
      == ButtonState.Pressed)
        this.Exit();

    string[] nameArray = new string[4];
    nameArray[0] = "Alexander";
    nameArray[1] = "William";
    nameArray[2] = "Molly";
    nameArray[3] = "Mary";

    nameArray[9] = "Jerry";

    base.Update(gameTime);
}
```

Here an array named nameArray is defined. The array has been defined as being able to store a maximum of five items (e.g., at index positions 0 − 4). However, the last statement shown in bold attempts to access an array element that is outside the range supported by the array, generating an IndexOutOfRangeException runtime error, as shown in Figure 11.21.

The occurrence of this runtime error brings application execution to an immediate halt. Using a try...catch...finally code block, as demonstrated in this next example, you can trap and prevent the error from terminating the application's execution.

```
protected override void Update(GameTime gameTime)
{
```

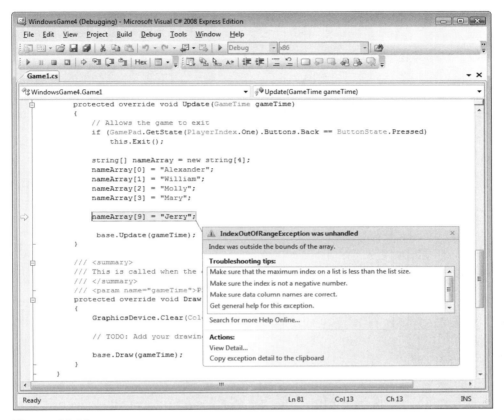

Figure 11.21
An example of an IndexOutOfRangeException runtime error.

```csharp
// Allows the game to exit
if (GamePad.GetState(PlayerIndex.One).Buttons.Back
  == ButtonState.Pressed)
    this.Exit();

string[] nameArray = new string[4];
nameArray[0] = "Alexander";
nameArray[1] = "William";
nameArray[2] = "Molly";
nameArray[3] = "Mary";

try
{
    nameArray[9] = "Jerry";
}
```

```
    catch (IndexOutOfRangeException ex)
    {

    }
    catch (Exception ex)
    {

    }
    finally
    {

    }

    base.Update(gameTime);
}
```

Here, the statement that generates the error has been placed inside the try block. A catch block is then added that executes if an IndexOutOfRangeException runtime errors occurs. Note that a variable named ex has been defined. This variable provides access to an Exception object that is automatically generated. The object's properties contain information about the exception.

A second catch block has been added to handle any other type of exception. The finally block will execute every time the Update() method executes, even if you fix the code statement so that the exception no longer occurs.

Hint

The order of catch blocks is important. If you have more than one catch block, always place more specific catch blocks first, followed by the more general ones because only the first matching catch block gets executed.

Trick

You can view a complete list of exceptions by typing catch in the code editor followed by a variable name and the keyword as, as demonstrated in Figure 11.22. Note that all exception names include the word "Exception" at the end of their name.

In this example, no statements have been placed inside the catch or finally blocks. As a result, no recovery actions are taken as would normally be the case. Instead, the application handles the runtime error by simply ignoring it. Although this example is admittedly simple, it does provide you with a template that you can use as the basis for creating more complicated exception handlers.

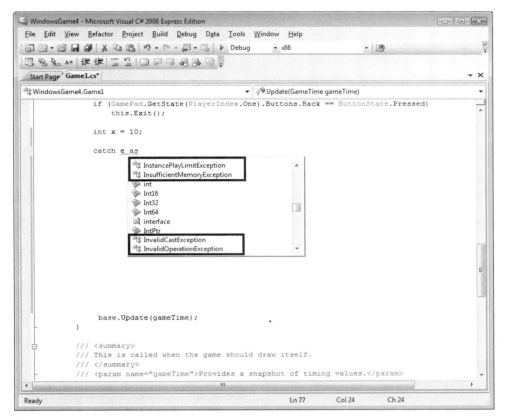

Figure 11.22
There are many different types of runtime errors.

Trick

If the likelihood of an exception occurring is relatively high, you should attempt to add new code to the application that programmatically handles the situation. However, if the chance of an error occurring is small but nevertheless still possible, adding an exception handler may be the way to go.

Summary

In this chapter you learned about a number of technical issues that you must address in order to deploy your XNA games to the Xbox 360 and the Zune player. This included making sure you provide for controls appropriate for each platform as well as address resolution and screen size issues. You learned how to work with conditional compilation symbols and to create platform-specific applications, as well as to convert your applications from one platform to another. On top of all this you also learned how to debug your XNA application, to set breakpoints, and to step through program execution. Last but not least, this chapter demonstrated how to create execution handlers in order to prevent errors from wreaking havoc on your applications.

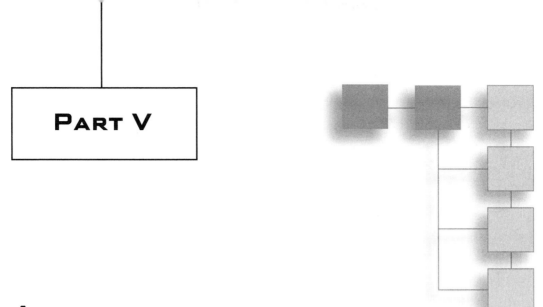

Part V

Appendices

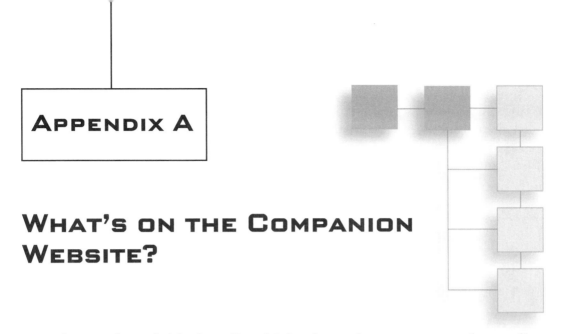

APPENDIX A

WHAT'S ON THE COMPANION WEBSITE?

Now that you have finished reading this book, you have a strong understanding of XNA Game Studio 3.1, and Microsoft Visual C# 2008 Express. You also have a comprehensive grasp of the basic principles involved in game development and programming. With this foundation now in place, you are well positioned to continue your game development and programming knowledge and skills.

To join the ranks of advanced game developers and to make your mark in the computer game field, you need to continue to learn, experiment, and most of all, you need to keep up on developing new games. There is a whole lot more for you to learn and to master than any one book could ever cover.

As you continue to experience and create new computer games, you will find yourself amassing a considerable inventory of source code and projects. You can use these projects as the basis for creating new and more challenging games, borrowing source code, and modeling new processes on existing ones. This way you won't have to spend a lot of time continuously reinventing the wheel every time you start a new project.

If you have been rekeying and running all of the game projects covered in this book then you already have a good collection of program code and sample projects with which to start. You should faithfully add to this collection every time you create a new game project. Over time, you will come to appreciate the benefits and time savings you will reap from this effort and will come to view these resources as an indispensible part of your developer toolbox.

Downloading the Book's Source Code

Without question, the best way to use this book is to re-create all of the examples that are presented and to spend time trying to improve and experiment with them. However, in the event you have skipped creation of one or more of this book's game projects, you can download the missing project source code along with any graphics files from this book's companion web page, located at http://www.courseptr.com/downloads.

Table A.1 provides a brief summary of all the game projects that you will find on the companion website.

Table A.1   Source Code Available on the Companion Website

Chapter	Overview
Chapter 5	XNA Template Project
Chapter 7	Input Collector
Chapter 8	Displaying Graphics
	Picture Viewer
	Electronic Picture Viewer
Chapter 9	Music Machine
Chapter 10	XNA Breakout

APPENDIX B

WHAT'S NEXT?

Congratulations on making your way to the end of this book. This represents a considerable accomplishment. You have developed a strong programming foundation that includes an understanding of how to program using Microsoft Visual C# 2008 Express and XNA Game Studio 3.1. You have learned not only the mechanics of working with the Visual Studio Express IDE but the basic principles of good game development. As a result, you have developed a strong foundation upon which to continue your game development education. However, while you have certainly learned a great deal, there is a great deal left for you to learn and experience.

To truly become a top-notch programmer and game developer, you need to keep experimenting, learning, and tackling ever more difficult challenges. To help you along your way and to make sure that you don't lose any of your momentum, this appendix provides a collection of online resources to which you can turn for more information about Microsoft Visual C# 2008 Express, XNA Game Studio 3.1, game programming, the Xbox, and the Zune portable media player.

Locating XNA Resources Online

A lot of information about XNA Game Studio 3.1 is available on the internet if you know where to look for it. To help you get started, this appendix provides a list of essential websites that you should frequent regularly in order to keep abreast of the latest information on XNA Game Studio 3.1.

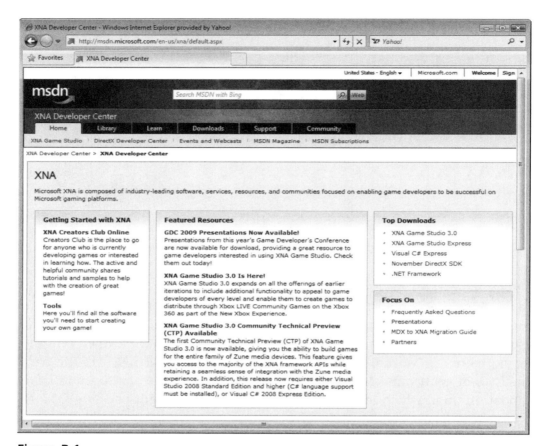

Figure B.1
You should visit the XNA Developer Center web page regularly to stay abreast of the latest happenings
with XNA.

The XNA Developer Center Website

The XNA Developer Center website (http://msdn.microsoft.com/en-us/xna/
default.aspx), shown in Figure B.1, is the definitive authority for serious game
developers. Here you will find information on XNA and get easy access to XNA
blogs and other resources.

The Wikipedia Microsoft XNA Page

The Wikipedia Microsoft XNA page, shown in Figure B.2, is located at http://
en.wikipedia.org/wiki/Microsoft_XNA. It provides a good overview of Microsoft
XNA and is a great source of references and links to online content, including
articles, tutorials, and online reviews.

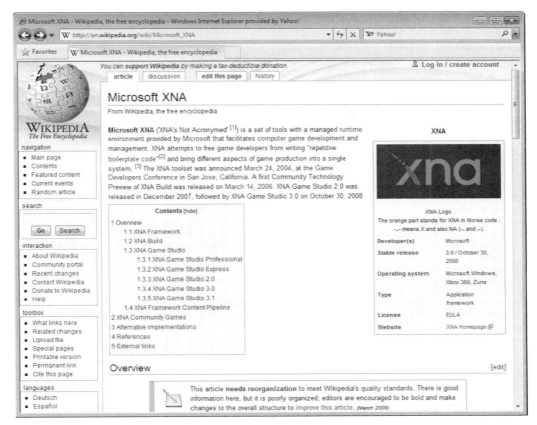

Figure B.2
The Wikipedia Microsoft XNA page is developed and maintained by a world wide community of game developers dedicated to sharing information about XNA.

The xnPlay Website

The xnPlay website, shown in Figure B.3, is located at http://www.xnplay.co.uk/. It provides visitors with previews of new Xbox 360 Community games. It is managed by a group of self-described game fanatics who love to play, talk, and share information about games. In addition to describing game features, this site also allows users to submit their own input.

The XBLA and XNA Ratings Page

If you want to keep your eye on what the competition is doing, a good place to regularly visit is the XBLA & XBLIG Ratings page located at http://xblratings .com, as shown in Figure B.4.

Figure B.3
If you want to learn more about a new Xbox community game, visit the xnPlay website.

Figure B.4
Games can be found by searching through various categories or by using a keyword search.

Figure B.5
The XNA Creators Club Online is a Microsoft sponsored community dedicated to XNA Game Development.

The XNA Creators Club Online Website

Once you have created an Xbox game that you think is ready for release to Xbox live, you'll need to go the XNA Creators Club Online by visiting http://creators .xna.com/en-US/, as shown in Figure B.5. Here you will be able to sign up for membership and access game development resources.

The XNA Team Blog

Perhaps the best way to stay on top of all the latest XNA news and events is to regularly visit the XNA Team Blog located at http://blogs.msdn.com/xna/, as shown in Figure B.6. This blog is frequently used for new and upcoming announcements. An archive of postings going back as far as August 2006 places a lot of information at your fingertips.

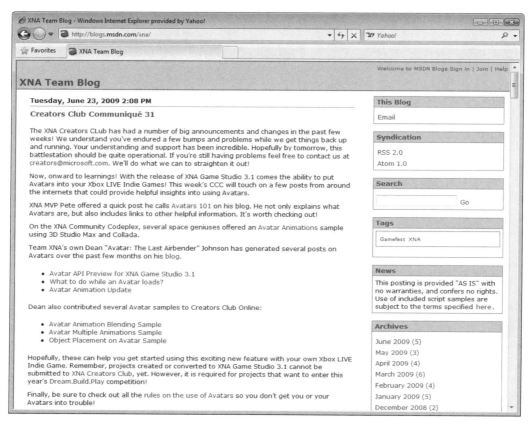

Figure B.6
The XNA Team Blog also lets visitors comment on blog entries.

The Forums Located at the Creators Club Online

If you have questions that you need answered or have information that you want to share, then visit the community forums page located at http://forums.xna .com/forums/, as shown in Figure B.7. As of the writing of this book, over 121,000 users had contributed a quarter of a million postings. To participate all you have to do is sign up for a free membership.

Locating Additional Information on Microsoft Visual C# 2008 Express

Learning how to work with Visual Studio or Visual Studio Express and becoming a good C# programmer is key to becoming an effective XNA game developer. In

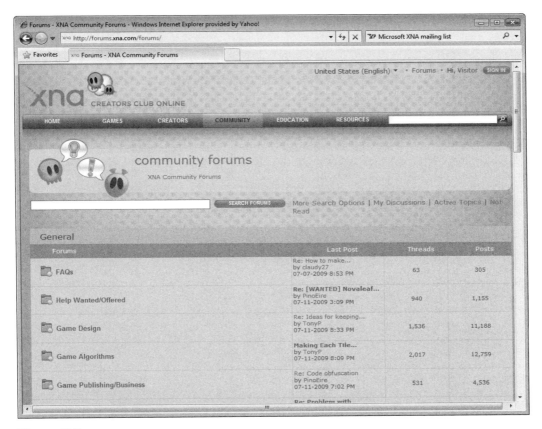

Figure B.7
The XNA Community Forums sponsor more than 20 separate form areas.

the sections that follow you will find several helpful websites where you can learn more about both of these topics.

The Visual C# Development Center

This book has provided you with a good overview of the C# programming language. However, C# is a topic worthy of multiple volumes. To learn more about C# so that you can take your computer games to the next level, visit http://msdn.microsoft.com/en-us/vcsharp/default.aspx, as shown in Figure B.8.

The Visual C# 2008 Express Edition Page

If you have elected to use Visual C# 2008 Express as your programming environment when developing an XNA game, then you will need to visit the Visual

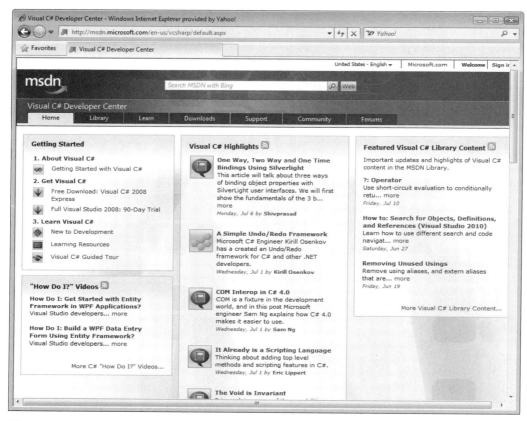

Figure B.8
The Visual C# Developer Center provides access to many different C# learning resources.

C# 2008 Express Edition page located at http://www.microsoft.com/express/ vcsharp/, as shown in Figure B.9. Here you can download Visual C# 2008 Express, watch videos, and access the Visual C# team's blog.

The Wikipedia C Sharp Page

If you feel you need a further review of C# or want to learn more about the language's origin and development, check out the C Sharp page (http://en .wikipedia.org/wiki/C_Sharp_(programming_language) located at Wikipedia (shown in Figure B.10). In addition, you will find links to dozens of other C# online resources.

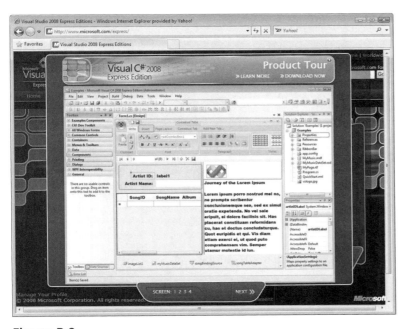

Figure B.9
Visual C# 2008 Express is free and can be used as a standalone tool for creating Windows applications or with XNA to develop computer games.

Figure B.10
Wikipedia's C Sharp page is maintained by a global community of C# programmers.

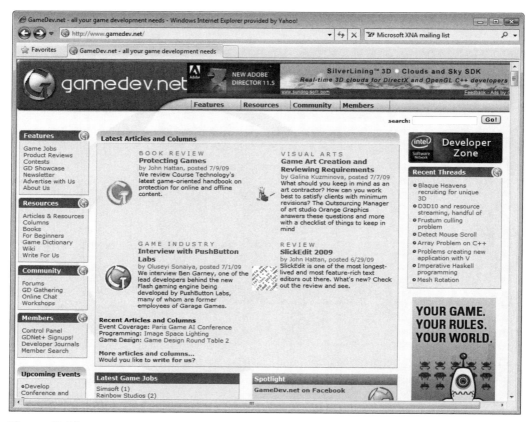

Figure B.11
The GameDev.net website is designed to address the needs of game developers.

Other Game Development Resources

Of course, there are plenty of other options for developing games than XNA. It's a good idea to stay abreast of alternative game development approaches and to become a part of the greater game development community. If you want to know more about game development, check out http://www.gamedev.net/, as shown in Figure B.11. You can sign up for a free newsletter, visit gamer forums, and learn about alternative game development frameworks and game engines.

The Xbox 360

While you can use XNA Game Studio 3.1 strictly to develop games that run on Microsoft Windows, you are missing out on a world of fun and opportunity if you do not leverage XNA as an Xbox 360 development tool.

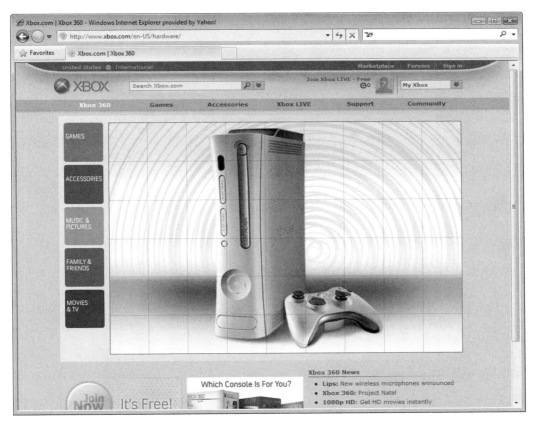

Figure B.12
The Xbox website is the definitive authority on all things Xbox360.

The Xbox Website

As far as modern gaming consoles go, Xbox is as good as it gets, both as a standalone device and as a network-based gaming platform. To learn more about Xbox 360 and to access a host of online resources, visit http://www.xbox.com/en-US/hardware/, as shown in Figure B.12.

Wikipedia's Xbox 360 Page

Wikipedia's Xbox 360 page (http://en.wikipedia.org/wiki/Xbox_360), shown in Figure B.13, provides an excellent historical record of the Xbox. Perhaps most useful of all is the abundance of links provided on this page.

Figure B.13
Wikipedia's Xbox 360 web page maintained by a global community of enthusiast Xbox 360 gamers.

The Zune Portable Media Player

Although not as robust or popular as the Xbox 360, the Zune player still represents a significant gaming platform for XNA. With the release of the next generation of Zune HD player in late 2009, Zune's new size and chipset provide it with video capabilities that surpass the iPod, while making it an even more attractive gaming platform.

The Zune Website

As far as modern portable media players go, Microsoft's Zune is at the head of the pack and with the introduction of the Zune HD, is poised to continue gaining popularity and market presence. To learn more about the full range of Zune players and their features, visit http://social.zune.net/, as shown in Figure B.14.

Wikipedia's Zune Page

Wikipedia's Zune page (http://en.wikipedia.org/wiki/Zune), shown in Figure B.15, provides an excellent overview of all the available Zune models and their features and capabilities.

Figure B.14
The Zune website is the definitive authority on all things Zune.

Figure B.15
Wikipedia's Zune website is maintained by a global community of Zune enthusiasts.

The Author's Website

If you enjoyed this book and are interested in learning about other game development options or other programming languages, visit my website located at http://www.tech-publishing.com, as shown in Figure B.16. While you are there drop me a message to let me know what you think of the book or how you think it might be improved.

Figure B.16
Visit www.tech-publishing.com to learn more about game development and to provide your feedback on this book.

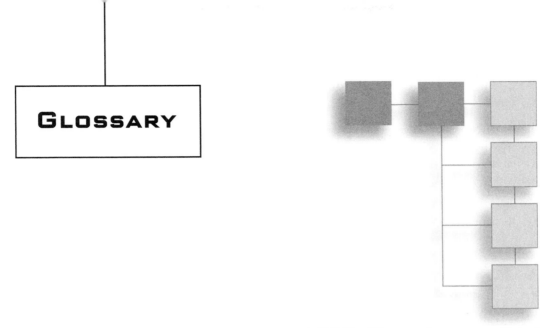

GLOSSARY

.mp3 (Moving Pictures Experts Group or MPEG). Files used to store digital music.

.NET Framework. A key component in most Microsoft applications that supports the creation and execution of desktop, network, and Internet-based applications.

.NET CF (Microsoft .NET Compact Framework). A specialized version of .NET designed for execution on Windows CE and which supports application development for the Zune player.

.NET Class Library. A large collection of classes that provides XNA with access to classes that define the different types of objects that can be instantiated (created) within applications and games.

.wav (wave). A compressed audio file that stores short audio sounds used to play sound effects in games and applications.

.wma (Windows Media Audio). A compressed audio file type created by Microsoft for use with the Windows Media Player.

Abstraction. The process of defining a logical representation of a class within program code.

API (application programming interface). An interface between application software and computer hardware that facilitates communication and information exchange.

Argument. A value, literal, or variable passed to a method for processing.

Array. An indexed list of values stored and managed as a unit.

Asset. A generic term that refers to different types of content used in games, including fonts, graphics, and audio.

Bitmap. A term referring to the format used to store graphic images.

Bounded collision. A collision that occurs when the `Rectangle` objects that contain sprites collide with one another.

Rectangle. An object used to contain and display a sprite.

Break point. A marker placed within program source code to signal the debugger to pause in order to facilitate debugging.

C#. (pronounced C Sharp) A general purpose programming language based largely on C++ syntax.

Class. A container for grouping methods and variables that work together in order to define all of the features and capabilities that make up an object.

Code editor. A specialized text editor that facilitates the development of program source code.

Code snippet. A template statement that you can insert directly into your program code and then fill out.

Collision. An event that occurs when rectangle-bounded objects make contact with one another.

Comment. Statements embedded inside a source code in order to document your programming logic.

Compiler. A program that translates program statements into machine code, resulting in a standalone application.

Compiler directive. An instruction that tells the compiler to do something.

Concatenation. The merger of two or more strings to form a new string.

Conditional compilation symbol. A set of characters that mark code statements that are intended for specific platforms.

Content pipeline. A mechanism in XNA that is responsible for converting game content to an internal format that XNA can use.

Constant. A known value that does not change during application execution.

Data. Information that your application collects, stores, processes, and modifies when executing.

Debugger. A software program that helps you to locate and analyze program errors and which facilitates the monitoring of status program flow and variable value assignments.

DirectX. A Microsoft Windows technology that facilitates the execution of high-end graphics and audio within applications and games.

Display overscan. An area on a television screen that is not used to display an application's output.

Dpad. A four-point directional pad found on a gamepad that allows for up/down/left/right input.

Encapsulation. The process used to outline the base functionality of a class and to provide the ability to interact with objects created based on that class through the properties and methods defined within the class.

Endless loop. A loop that runs forever, with no means of terminating its own execution.

Exception handler. A set of program statements that are designed to intercept and handle runtime errors.

Expression. A statement that is evaluated and produces a result.

Game. A standalone application that you can run and play.

Game engine. A framework that facilitates and simplifies game development by managing core game functionality and providing everything required to display graphic images, collect player input, and play various types of sounds and music.

Game library. A collection of files that serve a specific purpose and which can be used in the creation of games.

Gamepad. A game controller used by the Xbox 360 and also supported on Windows computers that collects player input via a series of buttons, thumbsticks, and a Dpad.

Game World Data. Data that is universally accessible throughout the application.

Game1.cs. A program file in an XNA application where you will make modifications and add code of your own in order to create your own unique applications.

Garbage collection. The process of keeping track of and removing unused resources from games and applications in order to make efficient use of system resources.

Global variable. A variable that is accessible throughout an application.

IDE (Integrated Development Environment). An application designed to facilitate the development of applications, which usually includes a code editor, compiler, and debugger.

Inheritance. The process in which one class is derived from another (parent) class.

Instantiation. The process of creating a new object based on a specified class.

Intellisense Everywhere. A Visual Studio Express feature that assists programmers in writing code by displaying suggestions on how to complete program statements.

Keyboard. A digital device used on Windows computers and the Xbox 360 to collect text input.

Keyword. A word, also referred to as a reserved word, that has a special meaning and purpose within a programming language.

Local variable. A variable that is accessible only within the scope where it is defined.

Logical error. An error created by a programmer mistake when developing an application's programming logic.

Loop. A collection of programming statements that execute repeatedly.

Method. A collection of statements that perform a specific task.

Microsoft's XNA Creator's Club. An online club whose membership is focused on the development of computer games developed using XNA.

Microsoft XNA Game Studio 3.1. A game development environment designed to help first time and advanced game developers create new generations of computer games that run on personal computers running Microsoft Windows, the Xbox 360, and the Zune player.

Mouse. An input device used on Windows computers that acts as both an analog and a digital input source.

Namespace. A mechanism used to categorize and group related classes.

NXE (New Xbox Experience). A new graphical user interface for the Xbox 360 designed to ease console navigation and introduce the use of avatars.

Object. A self-contained entity made up of methods, properties, and data.

OOP (object-oriented programming). A programming technique in which data and program code are managed together as a single unit in the form of objects.

Order of Precedence. A set of rules that dictate the order in which numeric expressions are evaluated.

Overloading. A programming technique in which the same method is defined two or more times, with each instance assigned a different argument list.

Parameter. A variable defined within a method that maps up to an argument passed to the method when called to execute.

Pixel (Picture Element). The smallest addressable area that can be written to or drawn to on the display screen.

Polymorphism. A term that describes the ability to define different forms of the same thing (in C# polymorphism is accomplished using a programming technique known as overloading).

Polling. The process of repeatedly querying a game control's state and processing its data.

Program. A text file containing code statements instructing the computer to do something.

Program.cs. The startup program for an XNA application.

Project. A container used to store and manage the resources and files that make up an application.

Properties. An object's attributes that describe some aspect of the object.

Runtime error. An error, sometimes referred to as an exception, that occurs because an application attempts to perform an illegal action.

Solution. A container used to store one or more projects that make up your XNA games.

Solution Explorer. A Visual Studio window that displays all the projects and files that make up an XNA game.

Source code. The code statements that make up a computer program.

Splash screen. A graphic that is displayed at the beginning of a game that is usually used to provide players with information about the game and how to interact with it.

Sprite. A bitmap image used to visually represent an object within a computer game.

Starter kit. A template that has already been highly customized to create a certain type of game.

Statements. The instructions that make up a computer program.

Step into. A debugging command used to execute the next statement in a program and then pause application execution in a program that has halted at breakpoint.

Step over. A debugging command used to execute an entire method in a program that has halted at breakpoint, pausing the application's execution before the execution of the next method.

Step out. A debugging command used inside a method to return to the calling statement where execution is paused again.

String. A set of characters enclosed within quotation marks.

Structure. A simplified means of defining and managing small collections of related data as a unit.

Syntax error. An error that occurs when a program statement is not formed in accordance with the rules of the programming language.

Texture2D. An XNA texture that supports the application of images on top of different types of 2D surfaces.

Thumbstick. A joystick control found on a gamepad that generates floating point values in the range of −1 to 1, representing X and Y coordinate data.

Variable. A pointer to a location in memory where a piece of data whose value may change during game execution is stored.

Variable scope. Refers to the location in a program where a variable is accessible.

Vibration. A means of supplying games with physical feedback in which a game controller is made to shake repeatedly.

Visual Studio. A powerful integrated development environment used by professional developers to develop computer applications and games.

Visual Studio Express IDE. An integrated development environment designed for new computer programmers and computer enthusiasts.

Wave. A digital audio file that stores uncompressed raw audio data.

XACT (Cross-Platform Audio Creation Tool). A powerful audio management tool that provides you with the ability to do things like edit sound volume and pitch as well as do things like create custom sound tracks.

Xbox 360. A next generation gaming console developed by Microsoft.

Xbox Live Account. A user account required to sign into the Xbox Live Marketplace.

Xbox Live Marketplace. An online store designed to support the Xbox and Xbox 360 gaming community.

XML. A markup language used to facilitate the exchange of structured data between applications.

XNA. A set of tools and resources provided by Microsoft that facilitates the development of computer games using C#, Visual Studio, Direct X, and the .NET Framework.

XNA Creators Club. An online membership that allows you to upload and make your games available for sale on the Xbox Live's Marketplace.

XNA Framework. A collection of game development tools and resources that facilitated the creation and execution of computer games on Windows, Xbox 360, and the Zune player.

XNA Game Studio Connect Game Add-on. Free software that you can download and install on your Xbox 360 that is needed in order to establish a connection between your Xbox 360 and your personal computer.

Zune Marketplace. An online location where Zune users can go to download more than 3,000,000 songs, videos, podcasts, games, and audio books.

Zune player. A portable media player similar to the iPod that is developed by Microsoft that plays music, video, and games.

INDEX